Pruning

BY DOROTHY and THOMAS HOOBLER

GROSSET
GOOD LIFE
BOOKS

PUBLISHERS · GROSSET & DUNLAP · NEW YORK
A FILMWAYS COMPANY

Acknowledgments

Produced for Grosset & Dunlap by Media Projects Inc., New York, N.Y.
Cover photograph by Mort Engel
Illustrations by Abe Echevarria
Photographs on pages 4, 23, 51 courtesy
U.S. Department of Agriculture. Photograph
page 91 by Tom Hoobler.

1976 PRINTING

Contents

1
Pruning Basics

Pruning is both an art and a science, dictated by what you want from a particular plant. For instance, a shrub like forsythia can be pruned so that it is thick and twiggy — to hide a garbage pail or form a hedge; or so that it is clean and arching — to trail over a fence. A grape vine is pruned a certain way for a good crop of grapes, but would be pruned like any other decorative vine if you were more interested in a shaded arbor. For this reason, this book has been organized in terms of your goals for a plant, rather than in terms of plant types.

The following chapter, Pruning For Structure, shows the training and pruning that is done where the branch pattern of a tree or large shrub is your major concern. Pruning for Foliage explains the pruning that is used to encourage a mass effect, as in many shrub plantings. Pruning For Flowers will give you the methods that encourage abundant or large blooms. Pruning For Fruit details specialized pruning that yields optimum amounts and quality of fruit. There is also a chapter on hedges, which require still another variation of basic pruning techniques; and on Special Effects — a few examples of particularly interesting or playful results you can achieve.

The organization forms some overlap. You will find mention of yews both in Pruning For Foliage and in Hedges; and of rhododendrons under both Foliage and Flowers. We feel this is practical for most home gardeners. You may be in despair about a straggly foundation planting this year, and only turn your energies to the bloom on your laurels after they have begun to look like dense shrubs again. You will find each plant cross-referenced wherever it is handled somewhat differently for different goals.

But there is certainly a science to pruning. To understand what you are doing, you will have to understand how a plant works. It is a short course in botany, but not a difficult one. Once you see how a plant works, it becomes common sense to see why this branch or that bud is removed from a plant to get new branches, more leaves, profuse flowers or heavier fruit.

So the plan of this book is botany first. Then the principles, techniques and details of pruning are derived from the botany in the context of the particular goals you might have in mind — strong and graceful structure, perfect foliage, abundant blossoms, plentiful fruit.

Plant Structure

Shape and structure are not the same thing. Although the shapes of different trees and shrubs vary widely, all have a similar basic structure. Knowledge of this basic structure is particularly important when your goal is the strength and pattern of branching in a tree or shrub. But even when your goal is heavy foliage or good blossoms, pruning instructions will use the terminology that you are learning here. As you come to recognize the parts of the framework of a plant, you will find it easier to know what you are doing when you get those clippers in your hands. Take your time studying this drawing, and come back to it again whenever you need to refresh your understanding.

Trunk: The *trunk* is the main support of a tree or shrub. When there are many supports they are called *stems* rather than trunks. The trunk is the space from the ground to the lowest main branch, a distance which is called "the height of the head."

Branches: There are four kinds of branches. The main side branches that grow out from the trunk of a tree are called *primary* (or *main*) *scaffold branches*. Branches that grow from the primary scaffold branches are called *secondary scaffold branches*. The dominant branch, which points skyward and is usually a continuation of the trunk or stem on either tree or shrub, is called the *leader branch*. *Lateral branches* on both trees and shrubs grow from primary and secondary scaffolds or from the leader branch. They are smaller and obviously not basic to the plant's supporting structure. Finally, all the branches growing from the end of any branch are called *terminal growth* to distinguish them from other laterals.

A few other special names are used to distinguish certain kinds of branches the pruner will need to know about. They are *suckers, spurs,* and *hangers.*

A spur is a short lateral, usually thick and with visible narrow growth rings. Spurs bear fruit in many species.

A sucker is a usually unwanted shoot that grows from roots, trunk or large branches. Watersprout is another name for any sucker that grows from a branch.

Hangers are branches that droop down, have slow growth, and are thin and weak. They are usually removed in pruning.

Canopy: The *canopy* of a tree is the whole area of branching — from the lowest scaffold to the very top of the leader branch.

Crotch: A *crotch* is the angle formed between two branches, between a branch and the trunk, or between two trunks. In general, a wide crotch is considered healthy because it offers better resistance to winds, ice storms and the weight of

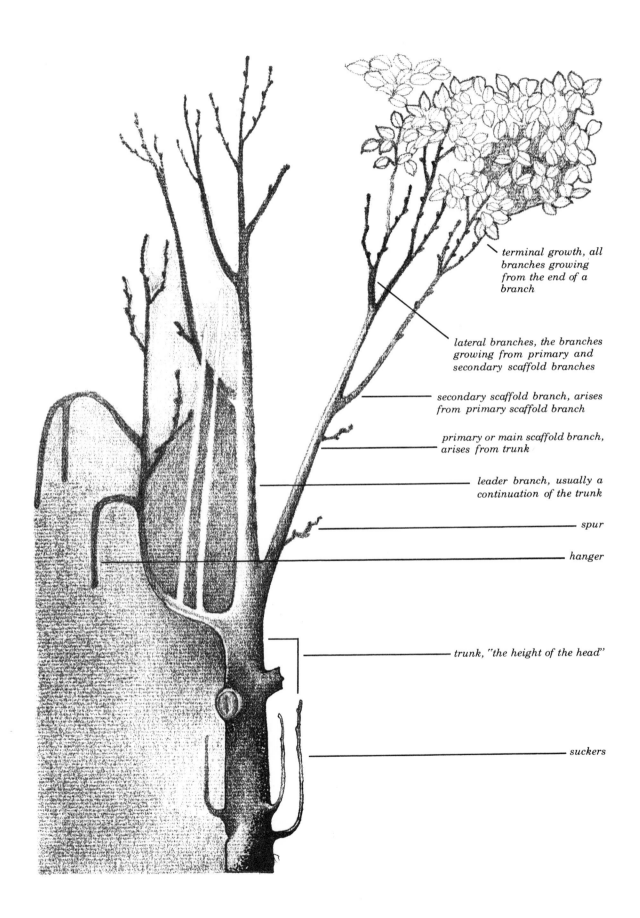

terminal growth, all branches growing from the end of a branch

lateral branches, the branches growing from primary and secondary scaffold branches

secondary scaffold branch, arises from primary scaffold branch

primary or main scaffold branch, arises from trunk

leader branch, usually a continuation of the trunk

spur

hanger

trunk, "the height of the head"

suckers

a heavy snow. Sharp angled or narrow crotches tend to collect debris and invite infection, besides being a weak point often split by storms. Narrow crotches are eliminated by pruning.

Plant Physiology

The Balance Between Parts

A plant needs light, air, food and water to live and grow. The three basic parts of a plant — roots, stems and leaves — cooperate with one another to take in and distribute water and nutrients from the soil, to manufacture food using the energy of light and the carbon dioxide in the air, and then to redistribute the food throughout the plant.

When the proportion of root to foliage is such that each can do its job best, a plant is said to be "in balance." No matter what your goal is as a pruner, keep this balance in mind as you work.

The roots of a plant not only anchor it in the soil, but absorb from soil the water, and the minerals dissolved in the water, the plant needs to grow. The leaves use the water and minerals from the roots, and carbon dioxide from the air to manufacture food for the entire plant. The energy to make the food is light from the sun, and the process is called photosynthesis.

The stem or trunk and its branches support the plant, of course, and by their structure also hold out the leaves to the air and light. But stems, branches and roots as well contain the circulatory system of a plant, transporting in conduits the water and minerals from root to leaf, and the manufactured food back throughout the plant.

In nature, a balance is struck between roots and leaves of a plant. If roots are damaged, some foliage and branches may die until a new balance is achieved. If a branch is destroyed, new foliage and new branches usually grow until the balance is righted again.

When you cut back or damage roots in transplanting, and so hurt the balance, it is often wise to cut back stems (and therefore leaves) or nature may cause leaves to drop or die.

When you cut foliage from a plant already in balance, the pruning encourages new growth to compensate for what you have removed.

Growth

More about pruning can be gleaned by understanding how a plant grows. Plants grow in two ways: branches grow longer, and branches grow

The only spots from which any branch can grow longer are the terminal buds at their tips. Every branch, no matter how tiny, ends in a terminal bud.

thicker. Growing longer is called primary growth. There is only one spot from which a branch, whether it is a huge limb or a tiny side branch, can grow longer: the terminal bud at its tip. If you look at a tree, you will see that every single unpruned branch and twig ends in a terminal bud from which it can grow longer.

New twigs and branches can also grow from lateral buds along the sides of branches. It is these lateral buds that give a plant a twiggy, full-foliaged effect.

Terminal buds produce a hormone that inhibits the growth of the lateral buds. If you remove a terminal bud, lateral buds are encouraged to grow. In nature, where terminal buds are left alone, they get the lion's share of food, and branches grow long to compete for light with other plants around. But to the gardener, a full plant may be more desirable than a long, leggy one, so terminal buds are often pruned to encourage side branching.

Growing thicker is called secondary growth. There is only one place from which a branch, stem or trunk can grow thicker: the layer of tissue just under the bark called the cambium. The cambium layer never grows lengthwise, so there is no way in which a trunk or branch can "stretch" in the middle. It can only thicken. This is important to the pruner mostly when he is interested in planning the branching pattern of a young tree or shrub, for when he decides to leave a branch that is growing at a certain height on the trunk, he can be assured the branch will always remain at that height. As the tree or shrub grows taller, the limb will not move with it. In other words, the branches you don't prune will always be exactly where they are now, and of course this will help you plan the ultimate pattern of a tree or shrub. Still more can be understood about pruning as you become familiar with each of the parts — leaf, root and stem — as separate organs.

The Leaf

As new branches emerge, leaves open along their length to manufacture food for the tree. By the process of photosynthesis, the leaves use energy from the sun to create sugar as food for the tree. The sugar is stored through the winter in the sapwood and roots of the tree, which explains where trees get the food they need for spring growth before new leaves can produce more food. In order for photosynthesis to work, leaves must have their topmost parts exposed to

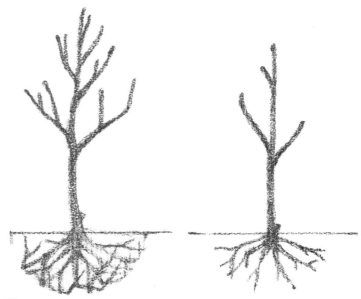

When roots of a plant are damaged, as they often are in transplanting, the plant's balance is restored by some of the branches dying back. The smaller root system is now able to support the reduced amount of foliage.

The pruner avoids "die-back" by doing nature's job. The top of this plant is first pruned back. Then, as new roots develop, new branches and leaves grow to replace what was lost.

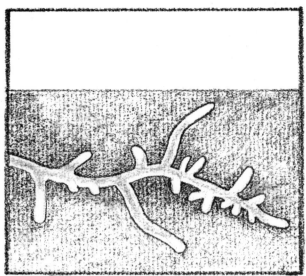

Of the entire structure of the root, it is primarily the thin, white feeder roots that concern the pruner. They are what feed the plant, and they are easily damaged in transplanting. Encourage feeder roots by pruning back lateral roots.

The only place from which a stem or trunk can grow thicker is the cambium layer just beneath the bark. It is the cambium cells that "heal" a wound in stem or trunk by growing a callouslike tissue over the cut.

light. And their bottom surface, which takes in carbon dioxide through pores, must have access to air. Nature helps by providing the plant with a hormone that tips the leaf toward the light. But that is not always a sufficient device when a tree is crowded with branches. Overcrowded branches are often removed to let in the light and air that helps the leaves feed your plant.

The Root

Pruning is sometimes used on roots as well as buds and branches. The root has three parts. The taproot provides an anchor for the plant. The lateral roots provide support too, and a broad structure from which the feeder roots can spread. It is in these feeder roots, in their tiny root hairs, that the water and minerals from the soil are absorbed for the use of the entire plant. The feeder roots, like branches, have primary growth tissue at their tips and are the fastest-growing part of the root system. They are constantly moving outward through the soil in search of new food. As with branches, the pruning back of lateral roots encourages more growth of feeder roots, and the result is a heavily-feeding fibrous root system that provides more nourishment to a plant.

The Stem

The stem or trunk of trees and many shrubs is made up of the bark, cambium, sapwood and heartwood. All of these parts perform important functions, but for the home gardener bark and cambium are most important. The bark is the wrapping of the tree and protects it from external enemies such as rodents, insects and some disease-causing bacteria. Breaking off branches or cutting with a dull tool injures the bark and opens up that much more area for invasion by insects and bacteria. The phloem, sometimes called the inner bark, carries the manufactured food from the leaves to the rest of the tree. Between the phloem and the central sapwood and heartwood is the cambium, which contains the secondary growth tissue. In order for a cut to heal, both cambium and bark (like skin) must grow over the wound. Cambium and bark cells cannot grow across the end of a stub, so when a branch of a tree is cut off so that a stub is left, the sapwood and heartwood center is never protected.

Insects, fungus and bacteria soon find their way into the tree itself. The sapwood of a plant is of concern to the pruner too. In the spring, some species of plants produce a copious amount of sap. Cutting into sapwood at the time the sap is flowing can cause such severe "bleeding" that the plant will be injured.

Pruning Goals

Pruning For Structure

Pruning can help develop a healthy solid framework for a tree, or an open framework for a shrub. Where the plant is not too large, judicious pruning can emphasize a pleasing pattern of branches also; or encourage low or high branching, as you choose. For the sake of any tree's health, you will want to encourage the development of strong branches, particularly the primary and secondary scaffolds that support the smaller laterals. The strong structure you achieve will help your plants survive ice, snow and wind.

Most damage to trees and shrubs is caused by weak, overcrowded branches and by the overcrowding of trees and shrubs that are planted close to one another. If your plantings are relatively new, pruning for structure now can avoid these problems before they are overwhelming. For instance, when you plant a baby tree and notice that young branches are crossing one another, you will realize that as the tree grows, those criss-crossed branches will rub against one another and injure the bark. It is easier to snip off one of the branches now with a hand pruner than to get the tree surgeon in when the tree is 50 feet tall. The same is true of a weak crotch, or even of a young limb that is not nicely placed. Pruning your shrubs on a regular basis can assure that the branches are spaced so that each will get the light and air it needs to produce full foliage and reach its own typical, interesting, mature shape. This sort of maintenance pruning to avoid problems is easy and can be fun to do.

If, on the other hand, you already have problems, pruning will have to be more drastic and time consuming — hard work in fact. It is also more confusing to know where to start and how far to go. Our advice is to begin with the obvious structural defects, as illustrated here.

1.
The first obvious step is to remove the dead branch on this tree.

2.
The narrow crotch is corrected by removing the scaffold branch from the leader branch.

3.
The forked branch comes next. Here the pruner must decide which of the two branches that form the fork is worth saving. Since one is a "hanger," and therefore weaker, it is chosen for removal.

4.
Next comes the criss-crossed branch. Again, a choice is made as to which to remove and which to save. The pruner may make an esthetic choice if both are equally strong.

When you can see that the basic structure of your plant is in good order, thin out branches where they are too crowded.

Pruning For Foliage

The typical amount of foliage a plant produces is determined by its variety and by the environment in which the plant is grown. But you can encourage increase in size and amount of foliage by pruning. Since leaves need to absorb the energy of light to "breathe" and the carbon dioxide in air to perform their food-making function, you can encourage the development of healthy leaves by removing branches that hinder light and air reaching the remaining branches. Too-dense foliage at the top of a tree or shrub tends to cut off the carbon dioxide supply and light to the lower branches, and this leads to straggliness. Thinning branches from the top will help.

Vegetative buds, as opposed to flower buds, are those that develop into new twigs, branches and leaves. They are usually formed on the branches which grew the previous year. The bud from which the branch is formed is the terminal bud. As the new branch develops and leaves are formed, a lateral or axillary bud is formed in the axil of the leaf and stem (the "joint" between them). This point on the stem is called a node. In many plants, lateral buds do not start growth at the same time as the terminal bud because the growing terminal bud inhibits the growth of the lateral ones. Removing the terminal bud induces the growth of lateral buds.

When lateral buds do not grow during the same season as the terminal buds, they are called "dormant." In addition, branches may have adventitious buds — ones that are not often visible, but which are "waiting in the wings," so to speak. Adventitious and dormant buds, like any other lateral buds, can both be stimulated to grow by pruning terminal buds.

So if you want a more bushy appearance to your plant, remove the terminal buds. If you want a tall and airy look to your plant, remove some of the lateral buds.

For a nice green look, you may want to snip off flowers that are developing, though flower removal isn't always considered as pruning. In some plants they are not particularly attractive, and they take away nourishment from the foliage. Removing flowers encourages the growth of vegetative buds.

The terminal bud on any twig or branch contains a hormone that inhibits growth of the lateral buds further down the branch. When it is removed, the lateral buds have a better chance to develop.

Pruning For Flowers

Flowers develop from either special flower buds or vegetative buds. Where flower buds are formed, you can recognize them by their round, plump appearance. They are usually larger than vegetative buds. The function of the flower is to produce the seed which will perpetuate the species. Nature is not often concerned that the flower be big and showy. Many flowers are barely visible. You, however, will want the most attractive flowers possible. Pruning is necessary in a few flowers — roses for example — to get the large flowers that many people value. Removal of some of the flower buds — called disbudding — channels more nourishment into the remaining ones. The result is a larger flower. In some cases you may not be concerned about the size of the flower, but want many small ones. Then remove few or no buds.

Pruning For Fruit

The function of fruit is to contain the seed that reproduces the species. Nature is not concerned with its high quality for eating or attractive color. But you will be. To get high quality fruit, you will have to prune the tree or bush or vine on which it grows.

Different kinds of fruit are developed in varying ways. Some fruits develop from the flower buds, randomly scattered about the tree or shrub. Others grow only on fruit spurs — short, stubby twigs that arise on fruit-bearing branches. In addition, some fruits will only develop from wood formed the previous season, others only on new wood. Knowing which fruits grow from what wood must be the real basis of pruning for fruit.

Sometimes nature provides more fruit than many stems can hold. As the fruit develops, you will have to remove some of it or the branch could break under the weight. The amount removed is determined by the species. The fruits that remain will receive a greater amount of nourishment and will be larger.

To ripen correctly, fruits need an adequate amount of sunlight. You can ensure this by opening up the structure of the plant so that good light can reach each fruit. Removal of non-fruit-bearing branches channels more food to the fruit too.

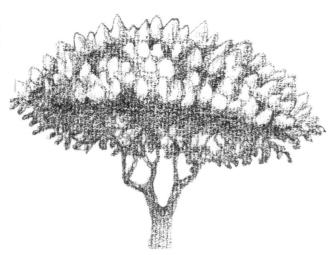

The size and number of blossoms on this lilac would be impossible without pruning. As soon as these blossoms are spent, they will be removed to prevent the bush from putting its energy into developing seed pods. Old wood that doesn't bloom well will also be removed to encourage newer wood to flower heavily.

Pruning Methods

Heading Back

One of the two main techniques of pruning is heading back. Heading back is cutting branches back to a bud, leaving a slight stub. Heading back produces a more bushy appearance because it encourages growth of lateral branches and leaves, increasing the number of stems and leaves per unit of space.

Thinning

The other major technique of pruning is called thinning. Thinning is the complete removal of branches back to a lateral branch, scaffold branch or the main trunk. In the case of shrubs, thinning refers to the cutting of stems to the ground. Thinning gives a plant a more open and spacious appearance without stubs. Plants vary in the amount of heading back or thinning they need but both techniques are used to some extent in all pruning.

Shaping

When both heading and thinning are used together to achieve a certain form for a plant, the technique is called *shaping*. Selectively you decide which branches or buds you will remove to develop or maintain a form for the plant.

One of the most important uses of shaping is to keep a plant the size that you want it to be.

Heading means to shorten branches of a plant by cutting them back to bud somewhere along the branch. It is usually done all over the entire plant.

Species and varieties of plants vary in the amount of shaping that you will need or want to give them. Sometimes you will shape mostly to keep the size of a plant within bounds. Sometimes you will want to thin and head a plant evenly to keep it symmetrical. Or you may thin and head unevenly to achieve an eccentric shape as an accent in your garden. The plant itself may determine how much shaping is possible, or when it can be done. The pyracantha, for instance, can be shaped into many forms. Other plants have a basic shape which can be accentuated, but not radically changed. Some varieties must be shaped while the plant is young and adaptable. Others can be shaped even when mature.

Carried further, shaping can achieve an artificial but pleasant artistic form. Espaliered trees which are trained by a very special shaping process are an example of an artificial form that adapts the plant to a particular environment. Espaliered trees are shaped to grow flat against a wall or along a fence, trellis or wires. A continual program of thinning and heading keeps them in a form that encourages fruit, and pleases the eye. Other examples of artistic shaping of plants are Oriental bonsai forms of evergreens and topiary. In topiary the artistry of three-dimensional shaping is seen in its most extreme form.

Thinning means to cut branches off at the point from which they arise—either at their joint with another branch, or where they grow from the stem or trunk. It is usually done more selectively than heading.

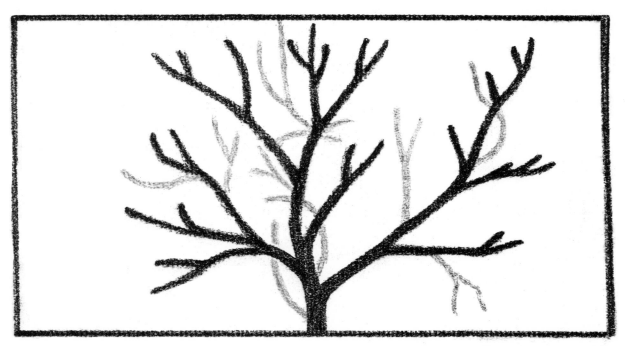

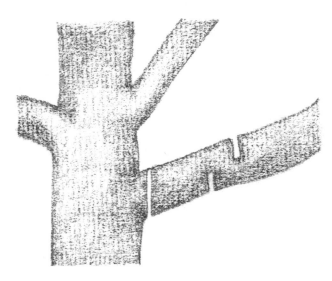

correct cut of limb on tree

pinching

Shearing

When heading alone is used, but is done with shears and in a wholesale fashion so that all the thin-terminal shoots are removed from a plant at the same time, the technique is called *shearing*. Shearing is used to keep hedges neat and in a formal pattern, and sometimes for formally-shaped shrubs as well. Shearing, of course, also shapes a plant, but the word "shaping" is used only to mean both heading and thinning. "Shearing" means heading without thinning.

Cutting

When a branch is headed — cut back to a bud — it should be a clean cut slanting away from the bud. In the illustration on the opposite page the first stub is cut correctly, with the slant away from the bud at a 45° angle and about ¼ inch above it. The second stub has been cut too far above the bud. The third is cut too close and the bud may be lost. The fourth stub's cut slants the wrong way. And in the fifth stub the angle of the cut is too sharp.

When a branch of a large shrub or tree is thinned — entirely removed — the cut is made nearly level with the trunk, stem or branch from which the cut branch arises. If a stub is left, it may eventually die; and the bacteria, fungi and insects that thrive in the dead wood can invade the plant. A clean, level cut will heal completely as cambium and bark grow over it. If the branch is large coat the wound with antiseptic tree-wound paint. When a stem is thinned, it is cut off level with the ground.

Pinching

Not all pruning requires cutting tools. An effective tool for pruning tender new shoots or buds is your own fingers. This sort of pruning is called pinching. Using your thumb and forefinger, nip the young tips of branches or buds to force side growth and make plants denser and bushier. Often you can see that a bud on the side of a branch will eventually grow into a branch where you don't want one. It is easier to rub the bud off now than to cut the branch off later.

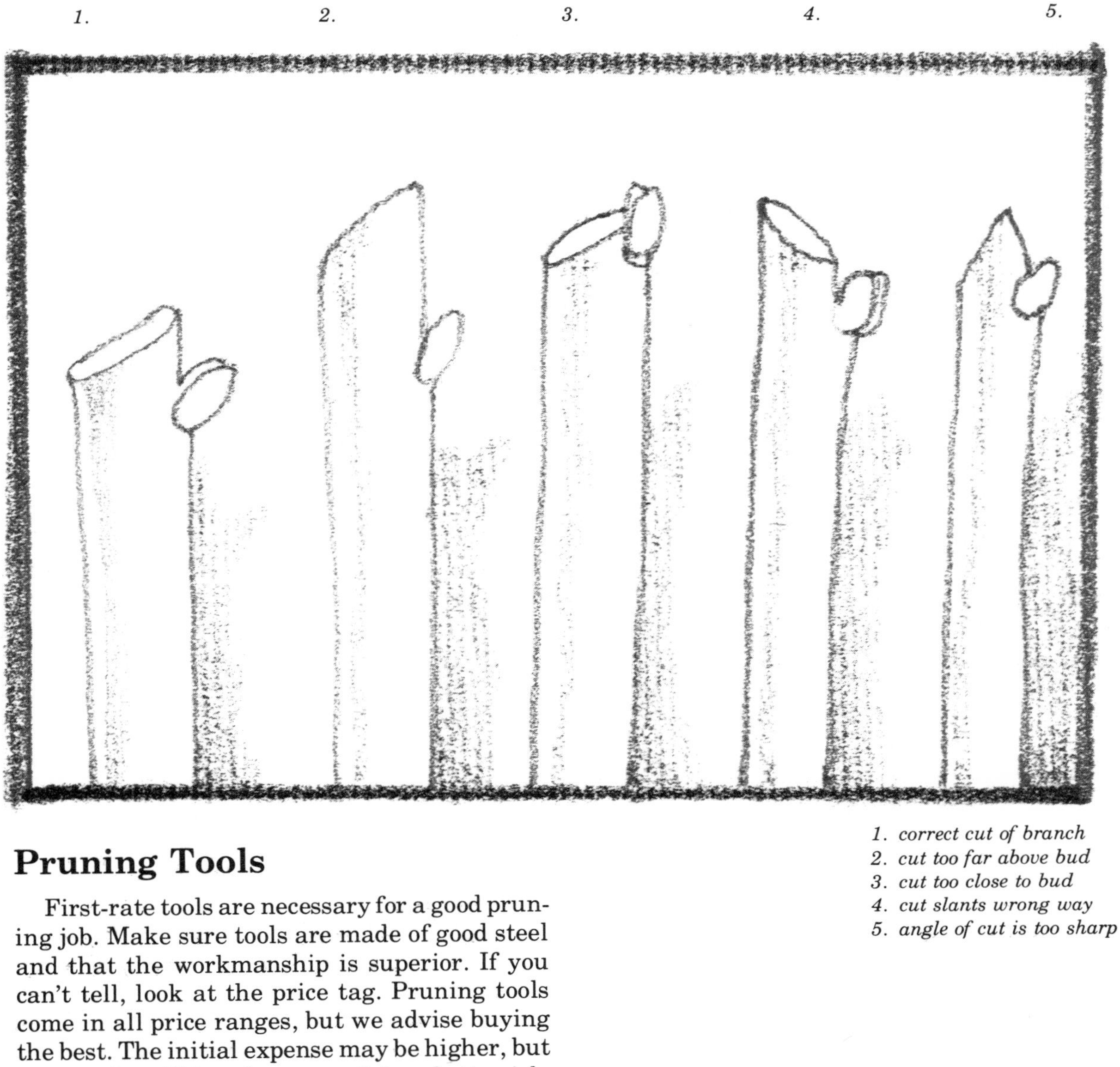

1. correct cut of branch
2. cut too far above bud
3. cut too close to bud
4. cut slants wrong way
5. angle of cut is too sharp

Pruning Tools

First-rate tools are necessary for a good pruning job. Make sure tools are made of good steel and that the workmanship is superior. If you can't tell, look at the price tag. Pruning tools come in all price ranges, but we advise buying the best. The initial expense may be higher, but good tools will last longer and do a better job. Inferior tools don't hold their edge and can spring out of shape while you are making your cut. They begin to tear and chew the wood instead of cutting it, and in the end are exhausting to your muscles and your temper.

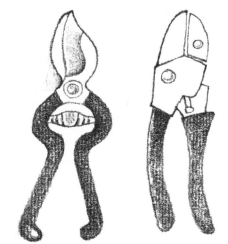

hook and curved blade and anvil-type hand pruners

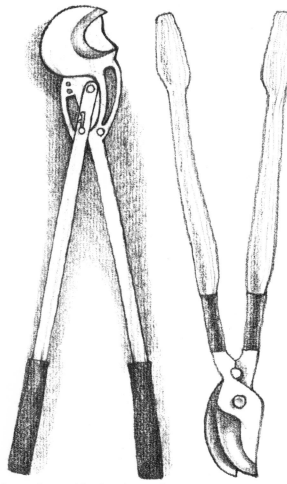

heavy duty and hook and curved blade-type lopping shears

Another thing to keep in mind when buying pruning tools is their compatibility with your strength. Pruning tools come in many sizes and with differently styled handles. Test the tool in the store to see if it fits your hand well and is light enough (or heavy enough) for you to handle comfortably.

Caring For Tools

First-rate tools deserve good care. They have to be kept sharp so they won't bruise the branches when cutting. Expert skills are needed for sharpening many of the tools, so patronize your local hardware store or garden center. You can, however, prevent rust from forming on the tools by wiping them after you use them with an oiled cloth. Keep all tools well lubricated with a light household oil squirted into the working parts too.

Hand Pruners: The tool you will be using most often for pruning is the hand pruning shears. Hand pruners are available in two main types: the hook and curved blade type, and the anvil type. The hook and blade shears have a tool-steel cutting edge that works in a scissorslike action with a thick hook for positioning and gripping the limb. When in prime condition, the hook and blade shears will make the closest and cleanest cut.

Anvil construction shears have a straight-edged blade opposite a flat bed of soft metal. Anvil shears are usually lighter than the hook and blade shears. But both come in different weights with different spring actions. Try them out before you buy to find the one most convenient for you.

Lopping Shears: Lopping shears are used with two hands. They are useful whenever you need the added leverage of long handles and where you cannot reach up to higher branches with a hand shears. They can be helpful when working in dense brush too, to save your hands from scratching. Lopping shears are provided with blades of both the hook and blade or anvil types of construction. An ordinary single-jointed lopper will cut branches as thick as 1 inch or 1¼ inches in diameter. For heavier branches, you can use a heavy-duty lopping shears with a patented power slot built in. When you need more cutting power with these shears, you simply shift the handles to the next notch to get both a wider "jaw" and added leverage. The handles of loppers come in a variety of styles — wood, vinyl or rubber-covered tubular steel. Lopping shears range in size from 15 to 35 inches long. Heavy ones can be very tiring and are not usually necessary. You will want to test the different kinds to see which one is right for you.

Saws: Saws are necessary for cutting heavier branches — thicker than 1½ inches —cleanly. If you try to cut a larger branch with shears or loppers, you will get a ragged edge that leaves the branch open to disease.

Do not try to use carpenter saws for your pruning. They will stick in the green wood of the tree because their serration and "set" is very fine. The pruning saw has special wide serrations, and the teeth are set at angles from one another to get a wide cut so the blade won't stick.

Pruning saws come in many different styles. The most common style is the curved saw with a rigid handle. This comes with a blade from 12 to 16 inches long. There is also a folding saw with a blade of from 7 to 16 inches long. This folds back into its handle. Both of these saws cut with a pulling motion.

The bow saw is also a popular tool. This can be hard to maneuver in crowded branches, but is light and cuts through green wood like butter. It cuts by both pulling and pushing. Many sizes are available with 15-inch blades and longer. Larger saws can be used for bigger jobs.

Hedge Shears: Hedge shears are just that. They should never be used for any other job than shearing. Shears are too large for the selective job of cutting individual branches. Some shears do come with an additional limb notch which is convenient for an occasional larger branch. In addition, you can get power hedge shears operated by electricity. These are only necessary if you have a lot of hedges or a formally-sheared foundation planting. The handles vary in length from 10 to 12 inches. Blades average 8 inches.

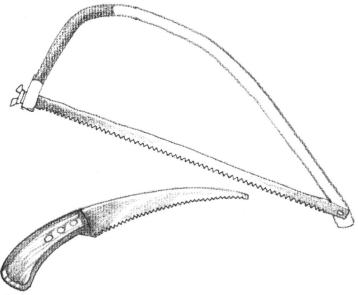

bow saw, curved saw

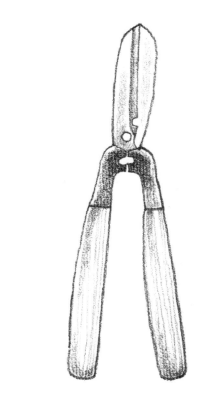

hedge shears

2
Pruning For Structure

Most pruning of trees and large shrubs for structure is done while the plant is young. The training they receive as babies can avoid much more difficult pruning later on as well as give you the shape you see in your imagination. Pruning older trees or shrubs for the sake of their branch strength or pattern is usually only necessary when some damage has occurred. This is not to say that this sort of pruning is all a tree or shrub will ever need. A fruit tree, for instance, is pruned for a particular structure while it is young, but still needs special pruning throughout its lifetime to keep it fruiting well. A large shrub like a lilac or some dogwoods may be pruned to have just the structure you want, but still need pruning to keep it flowering well. As you achieve the structure you wish for your plant, look up other pruning needs in the chapters on foliage, flowers or fruit. The very special structures of espaliers, pleached trees, standards and oriental conifers will be found under Special Effects.

Choosing A Young Tree Or Shrub

Finding a pretty baby tree or shrub at a nursery or seeing a picture of one in a catalog is not enough. The size and shape of that particular example, especially if it is really young, may tell you next to nothing about the same plant at maturity. Look to a good tree book or gardening encyclopedia to help you with the essential questions. If it's height you want, check not only eventual height but how long it's going to take to get there. Check for thickness of foliage; you may want dense shade, or you may want only a lacy foliage. If you are looking for a special shape, young plants may not reveal it to you, nor will knowing you want a maple be helpful. The species within a genus vary greatly from, say, the huge sugar maple to the red-leaved miniatures used for bonsai. The different members within a species vary as well. So when you think you have identified what tree or shrub you want, jot down the whole latin name: for example, *Abies balsamina nana*. *Abies* is the fir genus, *balsamina* added to it describes the particular species of fir (balsam fir), and *nana*, which means "dwarf," tells you that this is the dwarf form of balsam fir. The words added onto the species name often tell you the form of the plant — weeping, upright, dwarf and so on, or they may tell you the variety name, such as *hudsonia* or *sargentia*. Whether the description relates to form or variety, a good plant book will tell you what the plant will look like when mature if you look it up under its complete latin name.

If you get your plant from a nursery, you'll have a chance to look it over before buying. Be fussy. Check for foliage first if it's that late in the season. If leaves are yellowing, wilted or sparse, something is wrong and you shouldn't buy. If it's spring or fall, you can check to see that the plant is heavily budded. Next, check the structure. On narrow-leaved evergreens, avoid trees with sparse branching. The tree won't get any fuller with age. And sparse branching on any tree or shrub should make you suspicious; good nurserymen prune regularly for vigorous growth. Look carefully at the shape to see if growth is symmetrical. If it isn't, that's a sign the plant wasn't given enough space to develop fully on all sides. As you examine the structure of branches, keep in mind what you want of the plant. Even though you will prune somewhat when you get it home, the branches you save had better already be on the tree or shrub where you want them to be. Individual plants will vary in their habit already, so look for wide branching or narrow, arching or flat, according to the model you have in mind. Sometimes roadside nurseries tie their plants up and try to sell them that way. You must insist on untying the plant you're interested in and getting a look at it before you buy.

The last thing to check is the root system. Good nurserymen root prune several times before taking young trees or the larger varieties of shrubs from the ground to sell them. Root pruning develops the very fibrous root system without which the plant is likely to die after transplanting. If the plant is in a bucket or basket, it can be opened or the plant lifted out enough for you to see that the roots are hairy and fill the container well. The nursery may fuss more at opening a balled and burlapped plant, but will usually help you poke around enough to discover whether there are fibrous roots filling most of the ball.

This baby tree has been deprived of light on one side. It's a waste of your time to wait until it evens out. Don't buy it.

A young evergreen which has not been pruned may already be too straggly to bother with. Properly cared for, its branches would have been much closer together.

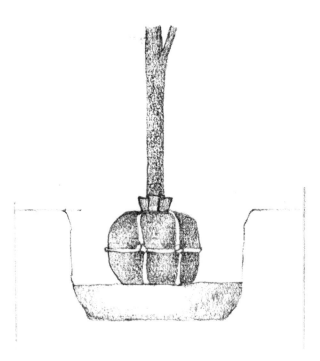

To transplant with the least damage to roots, dig the hole twice as wide and 1½ times as deep as the size of the root structure. Mix soil and peat moss in equal quantities in the bottom of the hole to raise its level somewhat. If any broken roots show, trim the ends cleanly with pruning shears.

Lower the tree into the hole (if it is wrapped in burlap, there is no need to do anything but untie it since the burlap will rot and roots can grow through it anyway). Check the height of the root ball; the trunk should emerge at ground level or slightly below.

Now fill in around the sides with soil and some peat moss, water the ground to a mush, and stamp down hard all around the tree, adding more soil as necessary. The peat moss will keep the soil friable enough for new roots to penetrate easily.

Training A Young Tree

The First Pruning

Any young deciduous tree, from an apple to an oak, is pruned back shortly before or after transplanting. The larger deciduous shrubs that you may decide to prune for particular structure, like lilacs, some dogwoods and magnolias, are also pruned back. Evergreens as a whole may not require this first pruning, and certainly pines must be left alone at this point.

Sometimes the first pruning of a tree or large shrub is done by the nursery before you buy it. But often the nursery, though it knows perfectly well the plant should be pruned when it is transplanted, has trouble selling a trimmed-back tree and will leave the job to you. You could prune your plant before you transplant it if the branches make it hard to manage, but most people's judgment is improved by seeing it in its actual location first.

After transplanting you are ready for the first pruning of your young plant. This pruning will be less for the structure of the tree or shrub than for its health. Since you know that some roots have been damaged in the transplanting, you know that some foliage (or budded branches) must be cut back to compensate. This first pruning will promote healthy new growth. Cut all the branches back about one-third, either heading to a promising bud or thinning to a branch that aims in the right direction. Remove any twigs that look ragged or have been bruised in transplanting.

The Second Pruning

The second pruning may be the most important you will ever do because now (and forevermore) you may be deciding the structure of your tree. We must humbly say that this is not true of a great oak or maple bought as a tiny baby, since its main scaffold branches are yet to be born somewhere way beyond your head and shears. But your dogwood, your lilac, your crab apple, Japanese maple, low-branched beech tree and even the bigger trees, if they already have good height, await the final choosing of your loppers. If you are doing the second pruning of a fruit tree, the special instructions will be found on page 24. You might also want to check pages 82 through 91 to decide if any of the special effects appeal to you before you make final decisions. Evergreens, both broad- and narrow-leaved, are rarely pruned for structure even when they are tree forms. Instructions for their treatment are on pages 38 through 43 in the chapter on Foliage.

As you follow these general instructions for most varieties of tree or shrub, keep in mind the normal habit of your plant and the vision you have formed of its fulfillment. You will be cutting off branches that interfere with your or nature's ideal and you will be leaving those that conform. For instance, nature intended most crab apples to branch low, but if you want picnics under the tree, you are going to prune the structure for higher branching. You will tend to favor branches that grow vertically if you want a vase-shaped tree, or branches that spread horizontally if you want a broad, flat tree. To get the best view, thin criss-crossed branches and other faults like narrow crotches, damaged areas, badly forked branches, hangers, suckers and awkwardly placed branches. Thin out laterals where they impede your view of the structure. Now stand back, or go away for a few days and come back to the job fresh. Find the branches that you know are winners in your design and keep them. Find the losers and cut them off. If the tree now begins to approximate your plan, do a routine heading back to encourage new growth.

In following years you may find new branches have grown where you don't want them, or you may change your mind and prune off one that you thought was going to work but didn't. Other than that, routine pruning of your tree — for as long as you can reach it — will only be a matter of taking out broken or diseased branches, some overall thinning to relieve crowding of lateral growth or correct the shape here and there. On smaller trees, you may routinely head back to keep the plant in good foliage (see pages 34 through 35), or prune to encourage blossoming (pages 50 through 65) or to achieve good crops of fruit (pages 66 through 75).

before   *after*

These before and after photographs clearly show the choices to be made as branches are thinned from a young tree. It helps if you know the shape you are after as you train the structure of your tree.

Training Fruit Trees

The structure of a fruit tree is more a scientific than an esthetic pattern. Strength of limb, circulation of air, sufficient light and the eventual height of the fruit for convenient harvesting are all considerations. The training may all be done in the second pruning, as with other trees, but will more likely take several seasons.

Fruit trees are trained at a young age in any of three ways. The first is the *central leader system*. In this system the tree is trained to one central trunk, and all the other branches are kept subservient to it. This is not a method often used today, because it develops the height of the tree when most people want low branches from which they can easily pluck the fruit.

The *modified leader system* is now used more often. It is similar to the central leader system, but fewer branches are selected and they are given equal importance to the central leader in the structure of the tree.

The third form of training is the *open center system,* in which the structure of the tree is entirely made up of branches, and the central leader has been removed. The advantage of the open center is more light for fruit production. But the disadvantage is that the structure is not strong enough for heavy fruit like apples.

Apple

The young apple tree is usually trained in a modified leader pattern. In the first few years the tree is encouraged to grow upright so that the branches will be spaced well. As enough branches develop to supply you with a choice, select from three to eight branches arranged spirally around the trunk. These are left to be the main scaffold branches, and all the others are removed. When you make your choice, be sure to mark for removal branches that form narrow crotches, because they will eventually tend to break under the weight of fruit.

Pear

The pear tree's structure, like the apple, is usually trained in the modified leader pattern.

To choose scaffold branches in your apple tree that are arranged spirally around the trunk, select the lowest branch first. Then walk about a quarter of the way around the tree until you get to a branch slightly higher and at least at a right angle to the first one. This is your second branch. Take a few steps more and repeat the process, always trying to select a branch higher than the one before, and at a right angle or even wider. Select from three to six spirally arranged branches and remove the rest.

But since the pear is by nature more upright and many-branched than the apple, more scaffold branches are left on the tree during this early pruning. The result is a much less open structure than the apple, even though the basic pattern is the same.

Peach, Nectarine, Plum, Apricot

Since the fruits of these trees are not as heavy as those of the apple and the pear, they can take the benefits of the open center structure. Choose low scaffold branches —only 3 feet or so from the ground. The leader is removed at this height, and the chosen four or five scaffold branches radiate out evenly from the center.

Cherries

Sweet cherry trees tend to be stiff and upright, somewhat like the pear tree. Their early structural pruning should be to the modified leader pattern. The sour cherry, however, naturally sprawls more, so that the open center system will work well.

Quince

The quince can be kept in its naturally shrubby form, or structured into a tree shape. Either form will yield a fruit crop, so the choice is largely esthetic. To prune for a treelike structure, select from one to three of the strongest stems. Cut all others off at the ground. Remove the lower lateral branches from the selected stems, leaving the upper branches to form a canopy.

Citrus trees

The early structuring of a citrus tree is aimed primarily at keeping the branching low and the tree short. At transplanting, cut the leader branch to 3 feet from the ground to begin an open center structure. The following year, select from three to four sturdy well-spaced branches that sprout from 2 to 3 feet from the ground and that aim upward rather than outward. Remove any branches that sprout below 2 feet from the ground.

central leader method of training

modified leader method of training

open center method of training

Restoring An Old Tree

If your trees or larger shrubs were never pruned for structure while they were young, or if they have not been much cared for, or if some damage has occurred, you may be faced with more drastic work than young plants ever need. Climbing big trees and lopping off branches is not an amateur's job. It's dangerous work, and though expensive to have done by a licensed tree surgeon, will still come out cheaper than hospital bills. However, if you need to cut off a limb that you can reach easily with a steady ladder, and you feel you are agile and well-balanced enough to not get the shaky hand syndrome while you are up there, here is how to properly prune a big branch.

First, decide if it is really necessary, since in an older tree or shrub no really big branches are going to replace what you cut off. If you think a narrow crotch, like a forked trunk, should be corrected, remember that by now it is supporting half the canopy of the tree and the tree will look maimed without it. If it's just a crooked or rubbing branch, or one too low for your convenience, you are probably right. And if it is a broken or diseased branch or a rotting stub, you are absolutely right.

Cutting A Limb

The first rule in making any cut at all with a pruning tool is that the cut be clean — not torn or jagged — or the wound can't heal properly. This is even more important when what you're cutting is a large limb, because the wound you leave is either on a main scaffold limb or on the trunk itself where danger of infection in the central circulation and support of the tree is a big worry. Check your saw by trying it on a log and get it sharpened and the teeth reset if it doesn't cut easily.

The second rule is that the cut be made flush with trunk or branch, so no stub is left to decay. Stubs will never heal. And the third rule is that the edge of the bark around the cut not be torn or crushed during cutting, since the bark and

The steps in cutting a large limb begin with an undercut 6 to 12 inches from the joint and only a quarter of the way through the limb. Next, cut the limb from the top just beyond the undercut, so that when the limb falls, the bark on the trunk doesn't tear. Last, cut the stub flush with the trunk or main branch. If the stub is large, another undercut may be necessary as an intermediate step.

cambium just below it can't grow to cover the wound if they are badly injured. Injured bark invites decay as well.

It is not hard to obey these three rules if your saw is sharp, if you are cutting a small limb and if you are doing it from a relatively comfortable position. The trouble comes when you are cutting off a large limb, for the weight of the limb as it falls tends to tear the bark below it, and the awkwardness of your position may make it impossible to cut flush as long as the branch itself is in your way.

To avoid these problems, large limbs are cut in three steps. First make an undercut about 6 to 12 inches from the place where the limb joins another limb or trunk. This cut is made only a quarter of the way through the limb you are removing. Second, cut the limb off a little further out than your undercut. The undercut will prevent the bark from tearing. The third step is to move in and cut the limb's stub cleanly, flush with the trunk or branch from which it has been removed. (If the stub is very thick, you may want to repeat the undercut as an intermediate step to be sure again not to injure bark.)

Treating The Cut

When the cut is finished, whittle the edges of the bark clean with a sharp pocket knife. To encourage healing even more, you can shape the scar to an oval with pointed ends — a shape the cambium layer seems to favor as it forms a callous over the wound.

The wound should now be painted with an antiseptic preparation, which keeps water out as it kills bacteria that try to get in. There are many preparations available. Some people use an asphaltum paint, others a special commercial tree wood paint. We recommend the latter, and also advise that shellac be painted around the edges of the wound where the cambium will start to form a callous to cover the scar before the tree wound paint is applied. Check every six months or so; reshellac and repaint if the area looks worn through.

To repair a hole in a tree that was caused by a decaying stub, clean out the cavity with a sharp knife until you have gotten completely down to live, healthy wood. Then coat the inside of the hole with antiseptic tree paint. If the cavity is so large you suspect it should be filled, call a professional to do the job.

This is the ideal shape of a wound that will heal neatly and quickly. You will have to do some whittling to get it.

Tree Chart

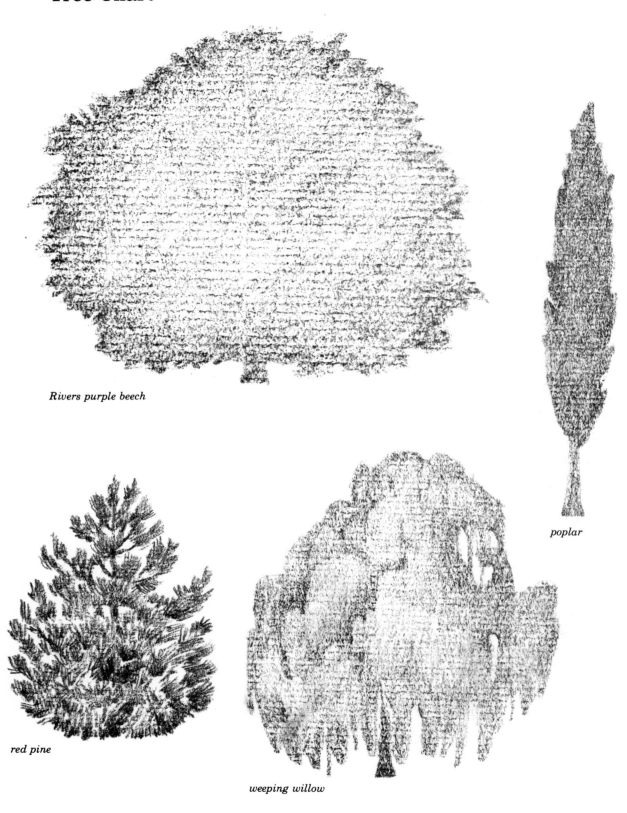

Rivers purple beech

poplar

red pine

weeping willow

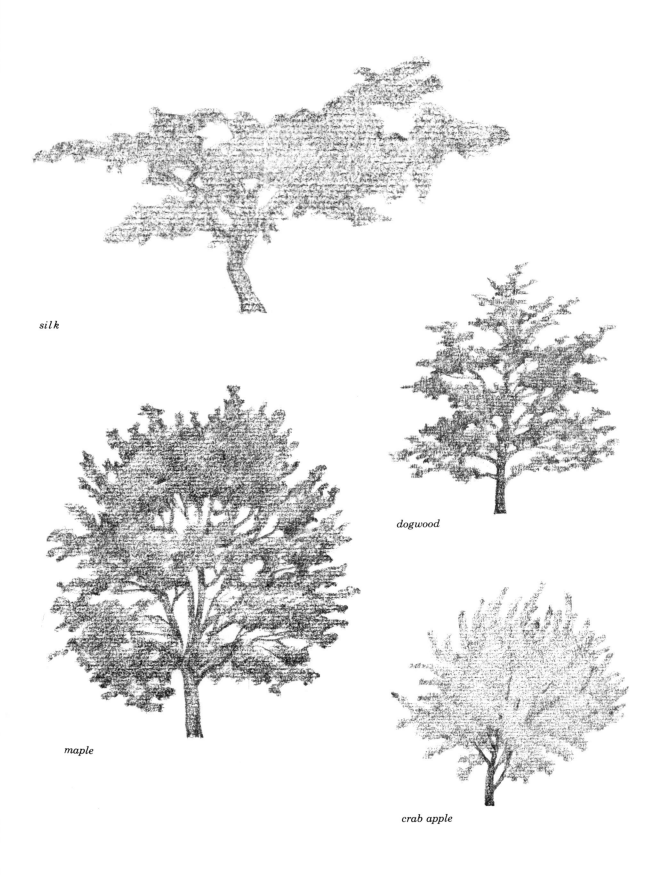

silk

dogwood

maple

crab apple

3
Pruning For Foliage

Foliage plantings are used at foundations to set off the architecture of the house with appropriate contours and interesting color, as accent points within a lawn, and as borders that define spaces in the home landscape. These foliage plantings are usually, but not always, made up of shrubs. Most narrow-leaved evergreens, for instance, whether trees or shrubs, could be considered foliage plantings as far as their pruning is concerned. You can use well-planned and well-kept foliage plantings to define different areas of your yard and garden.

On the other hand, nothing looks worse than a scraggly, out-of-control jungle near the house. This unfortunate condition can come about through lack of previous care, or poor planning. The person who planted your shrubs may not have planned adequately for the space they would need when they were full grown. Or they may be overgrown and overcrowded, because no one realized they should have been thinned routinely. Perhaps the plants have been trained to a formal style, which a later houseowner found too demanding to keep up. Or maybe they have grown leggy through lack of annual heading. The main problems with group plantings will be side growth, resulting in overcrowding of the plants; vertical growth, resulting in a straggly profile or a blocked view; and legginess, resulting in a bare look.

Before doing any cutting take a careful look at your plantings. What do you want of them? If you want a compact, mounded look, you will be doing either a lot of heading to get bushy growth, or shearing to get a formal look. If you want a more open, airy appearance, you will be concentrating on thinning, or you may want to remove a few plants that are crowding others.

To do all this, you will have to know something about various foliage plants. Some can be cut back to the ground and will send up vigorous new growth. Others should be reduced in size more gradually. Some are rampant growers and need either lots of space or lots of pruning, whereas others grow so slowly you seldom prune at all.

This chapter treats what to do with a neglected planting — one that has been pruned little, or incorrectly, or not at all. At the end of the chapter you will find an annual care chart that will help you understand routine maintenance pruning for a wide variety of the most common plants used for foliage effect.

Although foliage plantings can consist of both shrubs and trees, this chapter will be primarily concerned with shrubs. The botanist himself admits there is no sharp, precise distinction between shrubs and trees. The gardener, though, sees shrubs as short and having many stems, and trees as tall and having only a few or a single trunk. But when a plant is young, removing the leader shoot may start the development of the many-stemmed plant we think of as a shrub. And a plant that is normally a shrub can be trained to a single trunk by gradually removing lower branches and stems until a single stem supports the higher branches. In other words, it may be up to you to make your plant shrublike or treelike. With the possible exception of some of the narrow-leaved evergreens or shrubs that have been trained to look like small trees, few trees require pruning to encourage a normal density of foliage. On the whole, gardeners strive for foliage effects mainly in their shrubs and some evergreen trees, both of which are covered in this chapter.

The two major categories of foliage plants are the deciduous and the evergreen. Deciduous plants drop all their leaves annually at the onset of cold weather. The evergreens drop their leaves too, but not all at once so that they never have a bare appearance. Evergreens are of two kinds: narrow- and broad-leaved. As a general rule, deciduous plants are faster growing and therefore will require more pruning than evergreen ones, particularly the narrow-leaved varieties. But many shrubs — deciduous and evergreen — are perfectly fine with little or no pruning. If all seems to be going well and you like a shrub just the way it is, by all means leave it alone.

The winged euonymus is a twiggy shrub that, though it loses its leaves in winter, maintains interest by its decorative winged bark. Other twiggy shrubs like redtwig dogwood are chosen for foliage plantings as much for the color of their bark in the winter months as for the summer leaves.

A planting of a variety of narrow-leaved evergreens is compact and full all year long. But good foliage plantings often rely on contrast between foliage types rather than on a uniform bushiness.

Cleaning Up

What to Remove

Before you begin pruning, remove all debris and clean up around your plantings. This is the only way you're going to get a good view of the total effect to plan your pruning. Cut off all diseased and dead branches — or remove the whole plant if it is very far gone or altogether dead. Disease in one plant can spread to others and destroy whole sections of your foundation plantings. To see whether a branch or a whole plant is dead, examine the buds on it. They should be green and fairly smooth. If they are brown and withered, they are dead. Go down the branch and examine each of the buds. Cut back to the first live bud you find. If you have difficulty identifying the live buds, take a look at the tissue between the bark and the wood by making a small, sharp cut through the bark. Where the cambium is brown, the branch is dead. If there are no live buds, cut down the whole plant to ground level, or dig it out, roots and all.

After you have removed the dead and diseased branches and shrubs, it is time for a second look. If your shrubs are overcrowded, pick out the strongest and best to keep. Look for weak plants (or ones you just don't like) to dig out. Small shrubs or even young trees in good condition might be transplanted to another part of your foundation planting or garden. Now imagine what your plantings will look like without those weak or transplanted shrubs. You may find that this will solve your crowding problems. If it does not, you will have to simply pick your favorites in good locations to save, and remove the others even though there is nothing basically wrong with them.

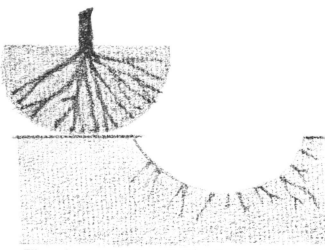

To remove a plant, cut down first to about a foot from the ground.

Dig all the way around it with a shovel, clipping or cutting roots with a hatchet if they prove stubborn.

When a shovel can raise the root ball from the ground, the plant should be easy to lift out and discard.

Digging Up A Plant

This method of digging up a plant applies to shrubs only, and only when you don't want to keep them at all. When you have a large tree to remove, get a professional to handle this difficult and dangerous job.

First, remove the top part of the shrub down to about a foot above the ground. You may need a saw to get through some of the older, thicker branches. Then dig a circle around the plant that you are going to remove as wide as the spread of the wider branches and as deep as your shovel. If the roots are old and thick you may have to chop through them with an axe. Try to rock the plant. If it still seems firmly rooted, ram your shovel or a crowbar deeply under the root system and try to pry it loose in several places. Now lift it out if you can. If it still won't come, tie a strong rope or cable to the shrub and pull it out, using the muscle of your car if your own muscles aren't up to it.

A young shrub that you want to transplant elsewhere is dug out much the same way — but gently. First prune it back somewhat by heading the branches, because you will damage some feeder roots when you dig it out and therefore some foliage should be removed to compensate. Now water the plant, both to keep the roots moist and to make the digging easier. Have ready a piece of burlap, a bucket or a plastic garbage bag to put the plant in after you've gotten it out. Dig the new hole in the place you want to transplant the shrub. Then take out the shrub, using the shovel to dig in a wide circle around the roots and snipping stubborn roots cleanly with pruning shears. As the circle is completed, push the shovel in deeply under the plant in several places to lift it. Usually you can now pick up the plant by its main stem to get it into the burlap or pail. Transplant immediately so roots don't dry out.

Cutting Down To The Crown

Next to removing a plant entirely, the most drastic thing you may have to do is cut a plant down to the crown. The crown of a plant refers to the stem area that is just above the ground. Though cutting down to the crown cures extreme legginess in some plants, it does not work for all. It should only be done with deciduous plants and only in the early spring or late winter. There is a good reason for this. When the leaves on deciduous plants drop in the fall, the plant becomes dormant. The manufactured food from the leaves is funneled down through the stem to be stored in the roots through the winter. If you pruned during the summer, you would only be cutting off the food supply to the roots. Next spring, there wouldn't be enough food stored and the plant could die. If, on the other hand, the pruner waits until the leaves have done their work, and the food is safely stored, this is what will happen: when the sap rises in the spring, it will be channeled into a smaller amount of growth, and rapid, vigorous, new branches and foliage will develop.

No amount of pruning can make up for lack of light or lack of food. If your foliage planting is particularly dreary, check whether light conditions are sufficient. Junipers, for instance, need full sun; if your planting is in the shade, you'd best move sun-loving plants elsewhere. How long has it been since you fertilized? If the answer is more than a couple of years, get some plant feeding advice from your nursery before you blame all deficiencies on faulty pruning.

This forlorn sight is a deciduous shrub cut down to the crown. New shoots will grow vigorously next spring. The case with some evergreens is different. Because they do not become fully dormant, they do not store up large quantities of food in their roots. If you cut them down to the crown there may not be an adequate food supply for the plant to put out new growth or perhaps even to survive. Cutting most narrow-leaved evergreens to the crown is likely to kill them, but the yew, on the other hand, responds well. Some broad-leaved evergreens like mountain-laurels, rhododendrons and boxwoods will be forced into development by such a severe pruning, but because it is risky, even broad-leaved evergreens are usually pruned more gradually.

Basic Pruning Sequence

As you will see in the more specific instructions for individual plants and plant types that begin on page 36, each specimen in your garden may have its own special pruning requirements. But you will also notice that these special requirements inevitably include some thinning, some heading and some personal esthetic judgments of your own. The basic sequence detailed below is intended as a general guide to where to begin, at what points to exercise judgment and in what order to take the steps that will result in a good pruning job.

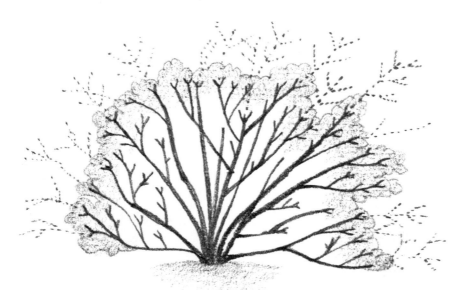

1. Now that your planting has been cleaned up, consider each specimen individually. Look up its special requirements at the end of this chapter. Consider: Does it have a pleasing structure that you would like to emphasize? Or has it a compact shape you would like to encourage? If you are pruning for a more open look, your first step will be to remove all criss-crossed branches on the outside of the plant. This will enable you to get a better view of the outline of the shrub. If you want a compact bush, don't remove the criss-crossed branches yet.

2. Use your hand shears to shorten straggly shoots back to a bud on either a compact or an open plant. You will have to look up individual plants to see how much further heading to do. If the plant requires heading, head back some of the current year's growth (or the previous year's growth if you are pruning in early spring) to get the approximate contour you want. If your shrub is vertical or open in habit, head back to the outside bud so the new branches will grow outward. For a bushy or horizontal plant, head back to the inside buds so growth will fill the interior of the plant. For very dense plants, like box, just head back and forget bud direction. Where there are three or more terminal shoots of about equal strength and you want to keep the plant compact, remove the center shoot. For very bushy plants, pinch off new tip growth all over the entire plant as well.

3. Now you will need to use your loppers for thinning. On any shrub remove those branches that have been forced down to the ground, because they are generally weak and often conceal garden pests. Thin the laterals for a more open structure if the interior growth is so dense that you're getting more twigginess than foliage, or if it will help you emphasize a structure you like. If your aim is a solid bushiness and your plant is thin at the inside and sparse at the bottom get tough with the dense laterals to the outside and top so the meager areas have a chance to grow—in other words, get rid of those criss-crossed branches now.

4. You now have your basic contour and either the open structure you wanted, or the encouragement to bushiness you wanted—all in accordance with any special needs or cautions about a particular plant. The pruning of your bushy plant is now complete; but you may want to go even further with your open one, and pattern the structure somewhat. Select the best branches and cut off the rest, trying to select for removal as many of the old shoots as you can without destroying the shape of the shrub. (See pages 20 through 29 for more discussion of pruning for structure.)

Twiggy Shrubs

Forsythia, box, pyracantha (firethorn), holly, the woody shrub-type euonymus, inkberry and cotoneaster are all examples of shrubs that tend to become twiggy and messy without vigilant pruning. In some cases, lack of thinning finally causes inside and lower branches to die out from lack of air and light, while in other cases the shrub simply looks like the tangle it is. With many twiggy shrubs, pruning is a general thing, and the pruner is free to choose whether he will prune for greater compactness or for a more open structure. With other twiggy shrubs, however, pruning is much more specific. If you can't identify a shrub you have, you can try to prune it by the general method recommended here. But if you know what it is, you will be safer to look it up in the chart at the end of this chapter.

Restoring The Neglected Plant

Begin by getting rid of dead branches by cutting them to a main stem, or dead stems, or to the ground. Prune away enough criss-crossing outside branches to get a good look at your plant. Now head back the entire plant — preferring outward growing buds if you want an open structure, and inward growing buds if you want a denser structure. On some really dense plants, there are just too many branches to bother choosing buds, but you could head a compact forsythia back to inward growing buds, while an arching forsythia would look better headed to outward growing buds. Now reach into the shrub with loppers or hand shears and thin out enough branches here and there to reveal the structure of the plant. Some of the branches you thin off will be ones you already headed back, and if that seems like a waste of time, it will not hurt to reverse the usual order in shaping and thin before you head. The only reason pruners often head before they thin is because they like to first establish a general contour for the plant, so that when they are thinning, they don't prune off a branch that helped maintain a certain contour. After some thinning, use your hand pruners to remove more criss-crossed branches and excess twigginess on the outside of the plant so that interior branches will get light and air. Of course, if your shrub is already full in the center, you can skip this last step. Now comes the big moment. Step back, consider

One choice you may have as you restore a neglected plant is whether to save old or newer stems and branches. Older branches tend to be both thicker and twiggier than newer branches. The bark may be rougher, and the color either duller or darker than new wood. Which of these two forsythia branches you save is an esthetic question. The new branch is cleanly arched, the older one is full of small laterals and will be bushy when in foliage.

your plant. Step in again and remove everything else you don't like, including any weak growth now apparent on the inside of the plant. Don't worry if your plant looks somewhat forlorn after this much shaping. The new leaves and branches will sprout soon enough.

Routine Pruning

From now on, pruning will be an occasional, minor version of the restoration job you have done. Head the shrubs in the spring when the new growth is just starting, still attending to bud direction as you pinch or prune. If you have a flowering shrub that blooms before June, wait until after blossoming to head the plant so you don't prevent flowering. Head lightly (not too many tips) for open structure; head heavily (most of the tips) for dense growth. Continue to remove dead and weak branches as you notice them, and to thin outside foliage so the foliage on the inside of the plant is encouraged. Complete the annual shaping by removing branches that sprout where you don't happen to like them.

Pruning Over-Vigorous Plants

Forsythia is an example of such a vigorously growing shrub that pruning has to be particularly vigilant. Faced with acute neglect, it becomes very tangled and a sparse bloomer. To correct, you can cut it back to within 6 inches of the ground in early spring, and still get several feet of growth the same summer — without blooms of course. To keep a forsythia under control, watch it carefully when it is in bloom. When you see a branch that isn't flowering well, cut it down to the ground right then and there. Forsythias grow so abundantly that those bright green vigorous shoots you see in the spring near the base of the plant will develop into long unbranched shoots by fall. If you prefer a twiggy, fuller look to your forsythia pinch these off after the shrub has bloomed. On the other hand, if your forsythia would look better with long, arching, non-twiggy branches, thin by cutting older branches down to the ground to encourage the newer growth. Such thinning has to be done at least every couple of years, and possibly every year. You can also head a forsythia somewhat, but excessive heading may cause suckers to grow from the axil between branch and stem, which you will have to cut off as they appear.

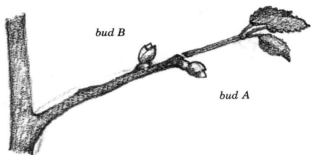

The top illustration shows the new outward growth that will come if the twig is pruned to bud A. It will help develop an open, graceful plant.

If it is pruned to bud B, the new growth will be inward-growing, and the plant will stay more compact and bushy.

Rhododendrons And Relatives

The rhododendrons, mountain-laurels and azaleas are all related. But rhododendrons and laurels are usually evergreens of the broad-leaved variety, while azaleas can be of either deciduous or evergreen varieties. All three plants have become popular in shrub plantings because of both their foliage and their bloom.

All three plants have growth buds under the bark all along the stem. So no matter where you prune (usually back to a lower side branch), you can encourage new growth just below where you cut. New growth is also stimulated by snipping the tips of new branches.

Restoring The Neglected Plant

When your rhododendrons, mountain-laurels or azaleas have gotten completely out of shape, drastic pruning can be used to restore the plant. In the case of all three, the plant can be cut almost to the ground, but be careful to keep the plant watered well afterwards. The dormant buds along the stem will send out fresh shoots. The safest and most productive time to do this radical renewal would be in early spring, when the plants are ready for new growth anyway. If the plant is not hopeless you can help cure legginess by less radical means. Cut back all branches by a third. Since either of these renewal prunings is done in the spring or late winter, when blossom buds are already set, do not expect any flowers from these plants this season. Next year they will bloom.

Routine Pruning

When rhododendrons, mountain-laurels and azaleas have not been neglected, there will be little routine pruning to do. Remove any damaged or dead branches as soon as you see them. Head back any straggly branches that interfere with the contours of the plant. Thinning won't be necessary. In fact, sometimes the plants will start to look leggy. If this happens, prune the branches back to lower buds or side branches.

For all these plants, be on the lookout for rejuvenation needs. Much of such plants' legginess comes with age. As stems get old they tend to produce little new growth. Cut the stems with the sparsest foliage back to the ground, or to the

Many rhododendrons sold today are new varieties grafted onto a sturdy rootstock. Be sure to check periodically for sucker growth coming up from below the place on the stem where the grafting took place. If these suckers are allowed to grow, they will produce inferior plants. Remove them by cutting below ground (to save your pruner blade, try to dig soil away from the sucker first).

lowest side branch or bud. You will then be promoting new growth for the plant.

Most of the pruning will be done just after the shrub has bloomed, so that you can enjoy this year's display but not allow new growth to go so far that it has already set the buds for next year's flowers. Pruned early enough, the new shoots that start will still have time to produce flower buds. But if you wait to prune later in the summer, you will not give the new growth time to produce flower buds.

When your shrub has grown as high as you want it to grow, pinch back terminal growth, again being sure to do your pinching on really brand-new tips, and not so late that the tips are in fact next spring's blossom buds. Pinching will give a bushier growth to your shrub.

Pruning Spent Flowers

Most people grow rhododendron and its relatives for the beautiful flowers as well as the attractive foliage. But these plants are all helped if once the blooming is finished, the dead blossoms are removed. This is particularly important with rhododendrons. On the rhododendron, the flowers open from a large roundish bud in the center of last year's leaf rosette. Just under this large bud are less conspicuous, narrow buds, arranged in a circle at the base of the flower stem. It is these buds that will be this year's new growth — and eventually next year's bloom. To encourage large new foliage, snip off the bloom as soon as it has faded, being careful to leave the leaf buds intact. Since the plant now cannot put its energy into the big seed pods typical of rhododendrons, that much more food will go into new growth. There is still another advantage to getting rid of the spent blooms. The new growth you are encouraging will begin to form the following year's flower buds earlier than the plant would have been able to had it been developing seeds. Your next year's flowers may be not only more plentiful, but larger. Though not as important, laurels benefit from this treatment too. Azaleas have so many blooms that the practice may not be profitable. More information on encouraging bloom in rhododendrons, mountain-laurels and azaleas will be found on pages 56 and 57.

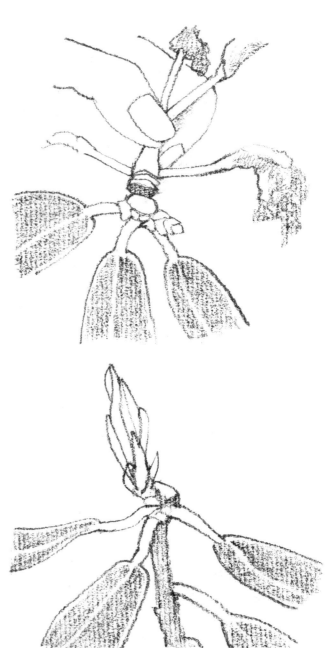

Blossom buds are fat and round, while leaf buds are narrow and more pointed. When rhododendron blossoms fade, pinch them off, being careful to leave the leaf buds undisturbed. If this flower is left to develop seed pods, the foliage will not start growing for another three weeks or more.

Camellias And Gardenias

Colorful camellias and fragrant gardenias are two other evergreen plants that, though their bloom is lovely, add full glossy foliage to the garden as well.

If you think your plant should be a little bushier, you can head by cutting branches back to where a scar marks where last year's growth began. The scars to look for are slightly thickened and of a rougher texture than the surrounding bark, and of course last year's scar is the outermost one. A cut slightly above the scar stimulates dormant buds along the branch and should give you bushier growth.

If your camellia has gotten very lank, it is a mistake to stimulate by heading severely. The heading will cause long straggly new shoots rather than short bushy growth. Fight meager growth instead with drastic pruning. Cut back through a few years' growth rather than just one year's. As new wood is forced to develop, attack it too, with vigilant pinching to shape the tree and constrain it to bushier growth.

Gardenias, like camellias, are appreciated for their compact foliage; regular pruning assures a bushy look. After flowering, remove the spent blossoms. Head the plant back uniformly to encourage new foliage and side branching. Where the shrub is overcrowded, some thinning will be required. This shaping process in gardenias is usually aimed at keeping the plant no higher than 30 inches, and broad rather than narrow in contour. Kept to this shape, you'll be pleased with both the compact foliage and with better flower production. (See page 56.)

Pruning Needle Evergreens

Needle evergreens, particularly conifers, are a special case in pruning for foliage, but not as special as most people seem to think. There is a prevalent belief that the conifers (cone bearers) are not pruned at all. The belief probably arose from the basic difficulty of pruning pine trees, which refuse ever to replace a branch once it is cut off. But even pines, and certainly all the other needle evergreens, can be pruned if necessary to keep their bushy foliage and preferred

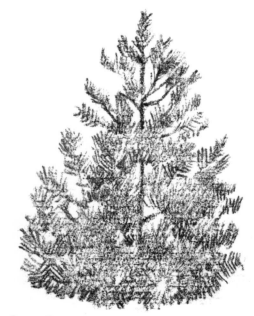

whorled pattern evergreen

random pattern evergreen

contour. Where space for their development is adequate, systematic pruning is not necessary for pines, spruces, firs and hemlocks. But if you think your conifer needs help, don't be afraid to tackle it.

Before you prune your needle evergreen, you will have to be able to identify the two major kinds: the branches of the first kind radiate out from the tree or shrub in whorls. These whorled evergreens are the pine, spruce and fir. The branches of the second kind grow on the trunk in random fashion. Examples of these are arborvitae, hemlock, podocarpus, juniper and taxus (yew). The difference between the whorled and random structure is evident even in the small shrub varieties of the plants popular in foundation or rock garden plantings. The Mugho pine, though squat in shape, still exhibits a whorled branching pattern. And even the most prostrate juniper branches randomly.

Routine Pruning

The whorled needle evergreens are pruned differently than the random growing ones. In the spring you will see at the end of each branch a short shoot covered with soft needles. This is called a candle. These candles reach full size in a few weeks and will grow no more that season. The only way to prune to encourage heavier foliage is to remove from one-half to two-thirds of each candle while it is still very young and tender. The candle-pinching will restrict the size of the tree or shrub and encourage new buds to form below the cut to develop into next year's denser foliage. With this kind of plant you can never cut back to old wood. It will not grow again.

On the random-pattern needle evergreens the growing season goes on all summer. The new buds are not only on the ends of the branches like the pine but are found throughout the branches on old as well as new wood. And since they continue to grow all summer, they can be pruned any time up until August (when new growth stimulated by pruning may not have time to "harden" before frost).

Pruning is usually light, and consists of occasional thinning for appearance and pinching back new growth to encourage bushiness.

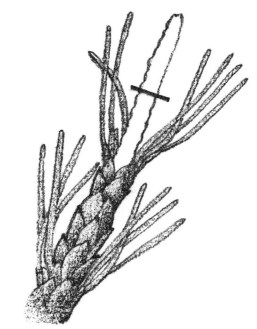

Whorled needle evergreens are pruned in early spring by cutting back the brand new "candles" by about half.

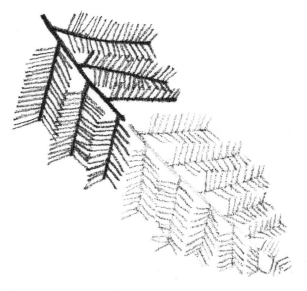

Random-pattern needle evergreens are pruned by pinching back all new growth throughout the tree by about half. The work can be done any time during the summer.

Junipers

Junipers come in a considerable variety of sizes and shapes, ranging from medium-sized trees to ground-hugging creepers. They can take plenty of pruning without harm, but the pruner is warned to put on gloves, as juniper needles are very sharp.

Neglected Junipers: For broad-growing junipers that have spread too far, choose branches that are invading your planting, trace them back to where they arise from the center of the plant and use your loppers to cut them off at that point. Use hand pruners to cut back outer branches into the semblance of the shape you're after. When this is done, step back and look at your plant. You may now see that there are gaps where you thinned out those first branches and feel you have made a terrible mistake. Not so. Simply choose branches that have buds or young branchlets facing the gap you wish to fill. Head these branches back to the right bud or branchlet. Each will then grow to fill the gap.

For vertically-growing junipers that have become too tall, you can safely remove about a third to a half of the plant, but it will be hard to avoid a lopped-off look if you shorten the plant a great deal. If the juniper has only one leader branch, you will be forced to cut it. Cut it to some point where another vertical branch is growing to take its place in the final shape of the shrub. If you are lucky there will be several leaders, and one will be low enough to suit you. Keep that leader and prune back the others selectively, trying to keep an eye on the shape of the shrub as you go. More timid, or perhaps wiser, pruners will decide to shorten their junipers over a period of several years rather than all at once.

Routine Pruning: When a juniper has reached the size and shape you want it to be, check its future growth by cutting back new growth almost all the way each year. This pruning should be done in the summer after the new shoots have had some time to grow and feed the shrub. If it continues to get out of hand, go back along any branches that need shortening and find a small shoot that closely parallels the branch. Cut just above this. By next summer the shoot will have begun to replace the branch you re-

Junipers and some other foliage shrubs have a particular problem with dogs; urine kills their foliage – and for some reason dogs seem to choose junipers to lift their legs against. You can't bring the branches back. Cut them off.

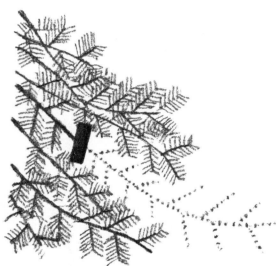

Cuts on junipers will not show if you cut a branch deep inside the shrub so the cut is hidden by other branches. If you fear a "hole" in the foliage, cut above a branchlet that is growing in the same direction as the old branch. It will soon fill in the gap.

moved, thus maintaining the shape of your plant.

Mugho Pines

Mugho pines are mounded in shape, slow growers and tufted with rather coarse, long needles. Some varieties grow to be 8 to 10 feet high, others only 2 or 3 feet. As a rule, it is unwise to prune much off any slow-growing plant, simply because it takes the plant so long to right its balance that the damage may kill it in the meantime. So even if your pine is long neglected, consider carefully before you head back branches or thin the plant. No branches or trunks will grow to take the place of ones you remove, so heading or thinning into old wood to shape the plant should only be done if you want to permanently change the form of your Mugho. You can give it a taller look by taking off lower branches; or you can judiciously rid the pine of branches that stick out and spoil its shape. The routine pruning that is done to Mugho pines to encourage bushy foliage is the same as for any pine. Each spring, "candles," young shoots of unopened needles, sprout from the tips of the branches. These are headed by cutting them half way down when they are still brand new. The result will be increased bushiness next year at the ends of branches. Removal of the entire candle will prevent that branch from ever growing longer, and this method is used to keep a branch a certain length forever.

Dwarf Needle Evergreens

The dwarf evergreens, particularly the dwarf hemlock, thuja and chamaecyparis are pruned little, if at all, mostly because their growth is typically so slow you wouldn't want to prune it off. If someone has sold you a "dwarf" that isn't, by all means prune it as you would other narrow-leaved evergreens (see page 40). But if it is truly a dwarf, shaping by removing branches that are out of the pattern you want, or heading them a bit, is the extent of the pruning you will need to do. Pinching new growth will increase bushiness, but a true dwarf will be as bushy as you could wish without pinching, and you will add to your own frustration by slowing growth even more.

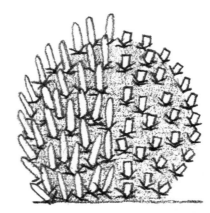

Pines are kept bushy by cutting their candles halfway down while they are still very young and tender. If you wait too long and prune after the candles are mature, you will be stopping all terminal growth at that point forever.

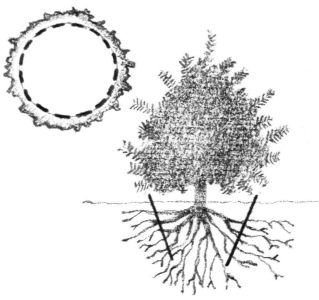

Young evergreens can be kept small enough for a foundation or border planting by root pruning. In the summer, mark off a circle around the tree at just the distance you want the branches to grow. Using a shovel, cut into the roots around the circle. Cut alternately, skipping one shovel width before making the next cut around the circle. In the following spring cut the rest of the roots by digging your shovel into the portions of the circle that you skipped last summer. This pruning will slow down the plant's growth much as a plant is dwarfed in nature if it happens to grow where its roots can't spread.

Taxus (Yew)

Taxus, or yew, are beautiful soft-needled evergreens of the family *Taxaceae*. Their versatility is shown by their varying sizes, some being used as a ground cover, while others reach a height of 15 feet if left unpruned. They have dark green, flat needles, usually ¾ inch long, that grow in such abundance that a yew's effect is often of solid foliage, with little branching visible. They can be grown as a formal or informal hedge, or they can be trained into many different shapes. We include the yew as a special example here because many homeowners are faced with disastrously-overgrown or grotesquely-sheared yews. Here is how to rescue them.

Shaping: Your first step is to plan the shape you want. Do not try to radically alter the natural habit of the plant — not because it is impossible or unhealthy, but because you and your shrub will be in a continual battle that the shrub is likely to win. If the present shape is so peculiar from bad pruning or shearing that you have no idea what nature originally intended, wait a year and see what the direction of new growth can tell you. To encourage an upright effect to your yew, first select those branches that seem strong and use them as leaders. Thin out thick lateral growth to emphasize the shrub's vertical direction. Then head back to outside or upward-pointing buds only. You can remove anything up to a third of the plant's growth.

To encourage a rounded shape, proceed in the opposite way. Head back strongly to get the shrub the size you want it, but this time to inside buds only. Encourage the growth of strong and numerous laterals by vigilant pinching of new terminal growth. As you shape the plant, thin only those branches that unbalance the look of the plant; there may be none, in which case don't thin at all.

To encourage a weeping habit, remove the lower branches of the yew and thin the remaining branches until the plant is quite open. Encourage lateral growth on those branches by pinching their tips. The weight of the lateral growth on these few branches will help them to droop from their own weight.

Pinching: Sometimes even in a well-pruned taxus you will get some straggly growth. If it is still very tender, pinch the young shoot back to

All yews are evergreens, and all have shiny flat needles along their branches. But beyond that, their shapes and sizes vary so widely that they have become perhaps the most versatile of foundation shrubs. They range from conical trees to low weeping shrubs. Since the pruner is usually the loser in battles against the natural shape of a plant, take a look at your yew and see if you can tell what shape it is trying to be. If you can identify the kind of yew you have by name, it will make it even easier for you to decide the type of pruning that is best suited for it. Try to find it in a catalog or garden book.

just above its hard wood. Or use pruning shears if the growth is too tough for fingers. This will foster bushy foliage in the shrub because it will stimulate the growth of buds in the wood below where you pinched. Many pruners pinch their yews routinely, whenever they feel the urge. If straggly growth is older and too hard to pinch, use pruning shears. You will have no difficulty in identifying the new wood in yews because the needles on this year's growth are bright green, whereas the needles on older wood are quite noticeably darker.

Shearing: To get a sheared taxus that has been neglected back into its original sheared shape, just shear it courageously. Yews can be cut back quite heavily, as much as a third of their size, though the result might look discouraging at first because the inside of the new shrub will be sparse in foliage until new growth begins. You might be less shocked if you can prune to the original shape more gradually. If you want to change the shape of your taxus—from a cone to a mound, for instance — lightly shear over it to approximately the shape you want and repeat when new growth gives you the opportunity. The most frequent problem with any sheared shrub comes from shapes where the top is wider than the base of the plant. No plant can be healthy and full-foliaged with such truncated shapes, because the foliage to the bottom and the inside of the plant is deprived of needed air and light, and you will have many dead or twiggy rather than leafy branches. To restore a badly shaped yew, remove dead branches first and then proceed to change the shape gradually by cutting the side growth at a slant inwards toward the top of the plant.

Some people object to the harsh lines of a sheared yew but still enjoy the formal shape. There is a solution. Once the plant is cut to the shape you want, keep it that way by frequent hand-pinching of new growth rather than shearing. The line of the plant will be slightly uneven but still true to form.

To undo previous shearing completely and get a yew back to its natural shape, first remove criss-crossed and overcrowded branches and thin the yew somewhat to encourage new foliage. Then let the shrub grow for a while until you can see what its natural habit is —vase shaped, weeping, conical or mounded. Then prune as with any other taxus, but expect the shaping to take several seasons.

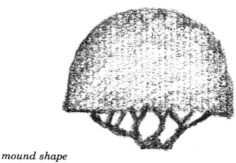

mound shape

truncated pyramid shape

conical shape

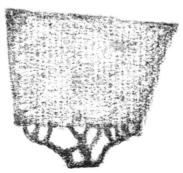

wrong shape

There are plenty of good sheared shapes to choose from, the only rule being that the shape must be smaller at the top, broader at the bottom. The last picture is unfortunately the shape most often chosen by the average home gardener. It is the one shape that can never be a healthy plant, because the lower branches are shaded and choked, and soon die out.

Vines

The foliage of vines has special uses to the home gardener not only because of what it looks like, but because of where it will grow. In fact, what defines a plant as a vine is its ability to hold fast to objects and surfaces, and grow along them. So vines are used to cover an ugly concrete block foundation wall, to climb an otherwise utilitarian light pole, to trace a pattern on a dull wall surface, to cover bare ground or rock with a carpeting of green.

Types Of Vines

It is helpful to the pruner to classify vines by how they hold to surfaces or objects, since that will help you know what vines are best for a particular location, as well as give you some guidance in a vine's early training. For instance, the simplest method for holding is when the entire stem of a plant twines vertically around a pole or tree. But nature dictates the direction of the twining, so that the Chinese wisteria will twine clockwise while the Japanese wisteria will twine only counterclockwise. You won't be able to change the plant's mind by all the training in the world, so this is a case in which the pruner gracefully lets the plant start its own direction before presuming to tell it what to do.

Other vines attach themselves with tendrils that twist about any object small enough for them to grasp. In the wild, small objects would most likely be twigs of nearby shrubs and trees. The function of the tendrils would be to spread the vine over other neighboring plants to hoard the sunlight to themselves. Grape vines attach by tendrils, and knowing this you won't make the mistake of planting a grape vine where it can grab hold of other shrubs.

The clematis is an example of still another form of attaching — the leaf stem itself is the twiner in this case.

Tendrils of other vines glue themselves to surfaces rather than twine or twist about them. The sticky substance on the tendrils of Boston ivy is what holds it to stone, brick and concrete.

Other ivies, like English ivy, and other vines, like euonymus and climbing hydrangea, have rootlike rather than stem-derived holdfasts. Certain points along the stem send out bunches of rootlets which dig into tiny crevices in rock, brick, rough concrete or rough wood — but you would have trouble convincing them that aluminum siding is an appropriate surface.

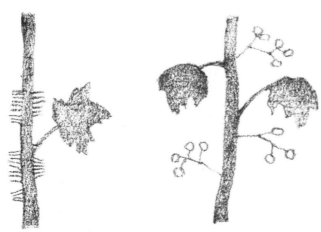

Before you try to train a twining vine, watch to see which way the stems twist. The vine on the left twists clockwise. The one on the right twists counterclockwise No amount of training can change the natural direction of a twiner.

Some tendrils, like the one at left, "glue" themselves to surfaces with a sticky substance. Others, like the ones at right, are rootlike and dig into tiny crevices in the supporting surface.

Shaping A Young Vine

If you want a vine to do what you tell it, start young. As the vines age, most become too woody and inflexible to maneuver into place. If you refuse to choose a vine that will cling to where you want it, you may have to build it a trellis (you can paint it the same color as the house wall if you like) or depend on the special training nails sold in plant stores. Wires are another unobtrusive solution.

When you transplant the young vine, cut it back to about 6 inches from the ground. As it grows snip off branches that sprout in the wrong places and help the right branches to attach themselves in the right places by using nails at least temporarily until the plant itself catches hold. Remember to watch for the direction of the twist if you're dealing with a stem-twiner.

Very formal foliage effects can be achieved with certain vines, such as English ivy, winter-creeper and Low's ivy, by stretching wires in a criss-crossed diamond or other pattern and forcing stems to grow along the wires. If you want less formal effects, the tracery will be a matter of taste — more pruning will tend to emphasize the tracery pattern, less will give you full coverage eventually.

Routine Pruning

Almost all vines tend to grow rapidly. Prune growth you don't want and dead or diseased branches and suckers any time. If the vine is long neglected and needs a lot of pruning or even cutting down to the ground, do it in early spring when the plant is still dormant. Otherwise, the new growth you encourage may still be too tender to get through the following winter. Thin vines, especially those like English ivy and euonymus that branch heavily, to let air and light into the foliage. The very bush vine you might favor will tend to die out less and harbor fewer insects if it is thinned from time to time. Head branchlets back as needed to keep the foliage vigorous.

It is safe to prune most flowering vines right after they have bloomed so you don't lose any of the display. If the vine blossoms in autumn though, you'd best wait until early spring to prune, to avoid tender new growth in the fall. More information on the special needs of vines planted primarily for their bloom will be found on pages 61 and 62.

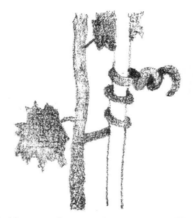

Tendrils hold many plants to their supports. This is the twining type of tendril.

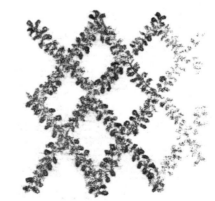

This diamond effect was obtained by running guide wires between short nails about a half inch away from the wall. The ivy is then trained along the wires. Copper wire may be your best choice, as it doesn't rust.

Routine Pruning Of Foliage Plants

Names	Kind Of Foliage	When To Prune	Reasons To Prune	Type Of Pruning
Abelia	evergreen or deciduous	spring	maintain size and form	remove old dead wood; thin every three years
Acacia	evergreen	after blooming	maintain size and form; control growth	thin to shape
Andromeda	evergreen	after blooming	maintain shape	remove dead stems and dead flowers
Aronia (chokeberry)	deciduous	spring to fall	maintain form	prune as little as possible; remove dead branches
Berberis (barberry)	evergreen & deciduous	late winter, summer	maintain shape	remove all three-year-old wood; head back for bushiness
Buxus (boxwood)	evergreen	spring, summer	maintain shape	cut back heavily; shoots sprout from old wood
Calluna vulgaris (Scottish heather)	evergreen	late winter, early spring	stimulate growth	cut back lightly; shoots sprout from old wood
Camellia	evergreen	after flowering	encourage flowering and maintain shape	remove all old flowers before seed formation; thin twiggy growth
Cassia	evergreen	early spring, late winter and after flowering	maintain dense shape	remove most of new growth
Chamaecyparis (false cypress)	evergreen	early spring and summer	maintain shape and stimulate growth	pinch branch tips to control growth
Cistus (rock rose)	evergreen	after blooming	remove old flowers	thin very lightly occasionally for form
Clerodendron trichotomum (harlequin glory bower)	deciduous	summer	maintain shape and flowering	do any needed pruning in spring; head back to keep bushy look; remove tall branches for shape
Cornus (dogwood)	deciduous	early spring	maintain shape and control size	thin for shape; flowering dogwood needs little or no pruning
Cotoneaster horizontalis (spreading cotoneaster)	deciduous	late winter, early spring	maintain size and shape	head back new growth if necessary
Cytisus (broom)	evergreen & deciduous	after flowering	maintain shape	remove dead wood; if plant gets into very bad shape, remove all wood that usually does not bud
Daphne cneorum (garland flower)	evergreen	after flowering	maintain shape, encourage bushiness	head back for bushy effect
Deutzia	deciduous	after flowering	maintain shape, encourage new growth	cut flowering branches back to strong side branches of new growth; cut oldest stems to ground to force new shoots
Dirca palustris (leatherwood)	deciduous	after flowering	to repair and keep good framework	prune as little as possible; thin old branches
Erica (heath)	evergreen	after flowering	for plant maintenance and shape	prune thin or diseased branches; remove faded flowers
Euonymus (spindle tree) (strawberry bush)	evergreen & deciduous	midsummer	maintain size and shape	remove old dead wood; thin for open structure
Forsythia	deciduous	after flowering	maintain shape and form	thin for more open structure
Fuchsia	evergreen	early spring	maintain shape	head back young branches to two buds; flowers bloom on new wood
Gardenia	evergreen	after and during flowering	encourage flower growth	needs little pruning; remove old and weak wood; thin leggy shoots when in bloom

Names	Kind Of Foliage	When to Prune	Reasons To Prune	Type Of Pruning
Genista (rock broom)	evergreen	late winter, early spring	encourage growth	to rejuvenate growth, cut old branches back to the ground
Hibiscus syriacus (rose of Sharon)	deciduous	early spring	encourage large flower growth	thin weak branches and smaller branches
Hydrangea	deciduous	late summer, fall	encourage large flowers	flowers bloom on new wood; cut old branches to the ground
Ilex (holly, inkberry)	evergreen	summer	maintain shape	prune sparingly; thin older, weak branches
Jasminum (jasmine)	evergreen	after blooming	to encourage flower and shape	thin old and outsize branches and head back for denser look
Kalmia latifolia (mountain-laurel)	evergreen	after flowering	maintain shape and form	thin for more open structure; remove faded flowers
Kerria japonica (kerry bush)	deciduous	immediately after flowering	to encourage new growth	cut back old branches to ground
Lagerstroemia speciosa (crape myrtle)	deciduous	early spring	to encourage new growth and flowers	cut back to ground old branches to promote flowering; flowers on new wood
Lavender	evergreen	any time	to repair plant	needs almost no pruning; cut flowers
Ligustrum (privet)	evergreen & deciduous	spring to fall	maintain shape	privets are usually sheared; shape during growing season
Myrica (bayberry)	evergreen & deciduous	after blooming	maintain shape	thin branches to maintain shape
Myrtus (myrtle)	evergreen	spring	maintain shape	thin to open structure
Philadelphus (mock orange)	deciduous	after flowering	to promote flowers and maintain shape	cut faded flowering branch back to bloom-free branch
Pyracantha (firethorn)	deciduous	spring	to control growth	to control growth, pinch young growth in spring, shorten long branches, cut oldest wood to ground
Rhododendron (rhododendron and azalea)	evergreen & deciduous	after blooming	encourage flowering and maintain size	remove blossoms; thin and head back to maintain good shape
Rosmarinus (rosemary)	evergreen	before flowering	prune leaves for herb use	remove flowers as they appear and cut stems for culinary purposes — this is sufficient thinning for good growth
Spiraea (spirea)	deciduous	spring, after blooming	for flowers and shape	takes severe pruning; cut oldest wood to ground in spring; after spring flowering, thin and head back; summer flowering varieties are pruned in late winter or early spring
Syringa (lilac)	deciduous	after flowering	promote flowering and maintain shape	remove old flowers and sucker growth; thin overcrowded plants
Taxus (yew)	evergreen	late spring, early summer	restrain growth and maintain shape	head back new growth by about half; thin occasionally; thin severely overcrowded plants
Thuja (arborvitae)	evergreen	early spring	maintain shape	shape early spring; remove straggly growth; prune again in summer to control growth
Viburnum (snowball)	deciduous	after blooming	maintain size and shape	remove old shoots every three years; cut to ground; thin weak wood
Weigela	deciduous	after blooming	maintain size and renew growth	cut faded blossom branches back to unflowered side branches; remove weakest branches at base

4
Pruning For Flowers

To get good flowers, you must have a generally healthy plant — one that is well-nourished and watered, and has enough light. But pruning can give the healthy plant a pleasing overall shape, more blooms and larger ones. As with plants that are grown for a foliage effect, flowering plants may have very specific pruning requirements. If you can't identify your plant, the principles explained here may be of some help. But if you know what you have, look it up by name in this chapter or in the chart at the end of it.

The first principle in pruning for flowers is that heavy bloom requires a good supply of light and air. Thinning to give the plant a light and airy structure that will encourage the development of flower buds is most likely done in early spring. The shrub or tree is thinned to allow light and air to reach all the leaves. Where the branches are too close together, they are thinned by cutting them back to a major stem.

The next principle also involves thinning but it is a little more specific and is done when the pruner can see flower buds already on the plant. A plant needs a good ratio of flowers to wood if its energy is to go into producing and nourishing the flowers instead of new woody growth. So the pruner may stop the straggly growth of weak, unproductive wood by heading back to buds, encouraging side growth. Many plants can also benefit by thinning the twigs that are without flower buds.

If you feel confused about the difference between a flower bud (one that will bloom) and a vegetative bud (one that will be leaves), remember that the vegetative bud is narrow and the flower bud is plumper and more round. Usually flower buds are also larger than vegetative buds.

If these few principles told you all there was to know about pruning for flowers, we would hardly need a whole chapter on the subject. Unfortunately, nature is seldom so simple. Not all plants grow separate buds for leaf and flower.

On some plants vegetative buds produce leaves, branches and flowers. And the flowers themselves may be located either in the axil of the leaf or at the branch tips.

And that's not all. On some plants flower buds develop on new wood, on others they develop only on old wood. As a general rule, pruning for flowers that bloom on new wood means you do your pruning in the spring to encourage the new growth. For plants that blossom on older wood, you do your pruning only after the tree or shrub has bloomed, so you have some hope of still seeing what you are doing.

Because of these complications, most of this chapter is devoted to the specific rather than the general. If you have looked ahead and already know that the plant you need to know about is not included, don't despair. Watch it for a year. Notice the pattern of how your plant blooms; it's sure to be similar to one we've talked about.

Disbudding

Another aspect of pruning for flowers is concerned with the size and shape of the flower itself. Many gardeners strive to raise large, perfectly shaped flowers.

However this type of pruning is different from simply encouraging the best natural growth of the plant. In nature the function of the flower is to produce the seeds that will reproduce the plant. Usually, large size and perfect shape is not a concern. If the flower happens to be a showy one, it is nature's way of attracting insects or birds. That this is also appealing to human beings is a coincidence.

The general practice in pruning for larger blooms is to remove some of the flower buds as they emerge. This is called disbudding. The remaining blossoms thus get more nourishment than they would have if none were removed. The flowers that remain grow larger than natural. If, on the other hand, you want many natural-sized flowers, you do little, if any, disbudding.

These flowering shrubs are kept well-thinned and yet they are loaded with bloom. Daring to thin enough may be the hardest part of pruning for flowers.

Flowering Trees

Flowering trees offer the gardener spectacular and even large blooms with little pruning. No one bothers much with disbudding simply because on a sizable plant it isn't worth the effort. The pruning of large flowering trees, as with any tree, is mainly a matter of pruning for structure (see chapter 2) early in the tree's life, while it is still your own size. From then on routine pruning is not demanding, although you often do have to pay attention to whether the tree blossoms on old or new wood.

Generally flowers that develop on this spring's new wood bloom during the same summer or that fall. Because they haven't yet set any flower buds in early spring, it is safe to prune them then. The new growth you encourage will increase the number of blossoms on the tree.

Flowers that develop on old wood (last year's or more) generally bloom during the spring. Here spring pruning is not a good idea, since you'll cut off flower buds along with the twigs. It is best to wait until flowering is finished. You will still encourage strong new growth, and presto! By next spring the new growth you encouraged will be the old growth that blossoms.

Magnolia

Magnolia is a common deciduous and evergreen genus that includes both trees and shrubs. They bear showy, sometimes fragrant blossoms that range in color from white to pink, to purple or yellow. Each flower appears at the tip of last year's terminal growth.

The most important pruning of magnolia is on the young tree or shrub. Like many other plants, you can select either one strong stem as a tree shape, or encourage several to get a more shrublike effect. (See page 82.) Even the baby magnolia is likely to give you a hint as to which it would prefer to be.

Once the young magnolia has been trained to the basic shape you want, it will need only light pruning and not necessarily every year. You may, if you like and if your plant is small enough to reach, disbud to get larger blooms. Then, during flowering, thin while the blossoms are at their height and use the branches for indoor decoration. Thin the blossoming branches you want back down to another branch and be careful not to leave a stub, since magnolias don't heal well and are susceptible to disease.

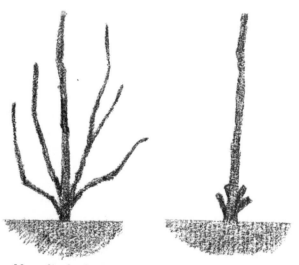

Magnolia shrubs are among those that can be trained to a small tree. The pruner tries to start with a shrub that already looks promising. This one has a major stem and several smaller ones. The smaller stems are cut to the ground, and the single stem left becomes the trunk of the little tree.

After blooming is the time to do any maintenance pruning, such as damaged or diseased wood and some small branches to lighten the structure if the tree is very overcrowded. Because of the magnolia's difficulty about healing, try to catch and prune branches you don't want before they get large enough to require a saw. On the whole, you'll be safer by thinning new wood rather than old.

Be on the watch for suckers. They are very common in the magnolia and should be removed early for healthy bloom and a clean-looking tree. If your magnolia is shrubby, you could let a few suckers grow if they look sturdy and attractive.

Ornamental Crab Apple

Ornamental crab apples vary in form from ones small enough to be grown in a pot to very tall upright trees. Pruning is mostly used to maintain a graceful open structure to the tree (see page 24). If the tree was trained as a youngster, you will already have the shape you want and can proceed as follows:

In the spring remove diseased and dead wood back to a sturdy branch, leaving no stumps. Then wait until after blooming to remove shoots that aim inward and crowded branches, cutting each back to another branch. Do this thinning only lightly, because while air and light are important, you don't want to encourage a lot of woody growth in a crab apple at the expense of blossoms.

Be sure to leave the stubby lateral branches (called spurs) on which the tree has blossomed. Like all apple trees, each year's bloom is carried on these short spurs. The last step, if your tree is still small enough, is to pinch back new growth that doesn't conform to the shape of the tree.

If the tree is in very bad shape you can remove up to a quarter of the branches flush with the trunk and thin the other branches as well.

Ornamental Cherry

The flowering cherries come in different varieties, some wide and spreading, some quite open in structure and others weeping all the way to the ground. The cherry blossoms bloom on wood produced the previous season, which means that as the pruner you will do this cutting after blooming. As a rule, ornamental cherries need little pruning if they have been trained to a healthy structure. (See chapter 2.) Thin to remove dead and diseased wood, cutting to lateral branches and leaving no stub. As the

Crab apples have been developed as much for their pretty shapes as for their heavy bloom. Nursery catalogs or a good tree book should tell you which shape a particular named variety will develop as it grows. Then when you prune, try to keep the ultimate shape in mind as you decide which branches to keep and which to cut.

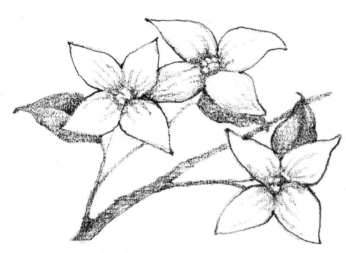

The petals of the dogwood flower are really specialized leaves, called bracts. The little nodules in the center of each bloom will become bright red berries in the fall. For this reason, spent dogwood flowers are not removed.

Lilac blossoms, on the other hand, develop into quite ugly branches of seed. The new leaf and stem growth will be retarded if the spent blooms are not removed.

tree blossoms you may continue to thin by cutting blossom-laden branches back to a lateral as well. Again, this is certainly not necessary every year. If the tree was not trained as a baby, or is so much neglected that major branches must be removed, try to keep your eye on what you are doing to the shape and structure of the tree. A space made by an overeager pruner may never be filled in.

Dogwoods

The flowering dogwoods are among America's most popular trees, and with good reason. The blooms are long-lived, the summer foliage is lovely and in the fall the tree turns to brilliant red leaves and clusters of red berries. Flowering dogwoods range from a medium-sized tree to a large shrublike form.

The dogwood trees need little pruning, since their particular appeal lies in their graceful layered form which nature achieves without cutting. The shrub forms need more pruning to keep them neat. Given a location in sufficient space and light, flowering should be plentiful without much interference.

Should your plant get twiggy and overcrowded, however, wait until blooming is finished before pruning, since all dogwoods blossom from last year's branches. Then cut out dead wood and thin mildly by cutting small branches back to a main branch. The thinning will help flower production if it has fallen off through lack of light to the tree. Don't remove spent flowers on dogwoods, because you will want to enjoy the bright red berries in the fall.

The shrubbier forms of dogwood tend to get more crowded than the single-trunked ones but you don't have to be nervous about heavy pruning. You can cut as many of the blossoming branches as you want. When convenient, go back to the shrub to cut out suckers.

The blooming vigor of shrub dogwoods eventually benefits by a rejuvenation. Cut out 5- to 10-year-old wood if you can identify it, and if you can't, choose those stems and branches that look thick and old to you. The new growth of younger branches will produce more flowers now.

Lilacs

Lilacs are enjoyed for their beautiful form and for their fragrant blossoms, both of which can stand a good deal of help from the pruner. If your lilac is very young, you don't need to prune it at all until it is four or five years old, except of course to remove dead wood. But if you want to prune it earlier, to train it as a tree shape by removing all but one or two stems, it won't hurt the plant a bit. (See page 82.)

When blooming is strong and the plant is established, you can start your program of pruning for flowers. The flowers on lilacs are formed on last year's wood, so watch it bloom before you start work. Then remove all the blossoms right away so they won't get going on the seed production that interferes with new growth. Cut the flower clusters just above the pair of buds which form where the top leaves join the stem. Now remove those suckers that lilacs love to send up from around their base. If you want to keep your lilac as a profusely blooming, many-stemmed shrub, thin out a few of the oldest stems down to the ground. It's safe to thin out a third of the oldest stems, because the newer stems will keep the bush healthy and full of flowers. If you have shaped your lilac as a tree, of course, you will be thinning by cutting branches here and there back to a main branch, and probably shaping the canopy of the tree by some heading as well.

If your lilac is way overgrown and no longer productive, more drastic action can be taken. Don't wait 'til blossom time. Prune in early spring by cutting all the stems down to 18 inches from the ground to promote the new bush growth that will flower the next or the following year. This should only be done on lilacs grown on their own roots. Grafted plants (look for the telltale bump just above the soil) don't have the strength for drastic rejuvenation.

Camellias

Camellias are versatile evergreen plants that can be trained into trees, shrubs or hedges. Since the camellia blooms on wood developed the previous year, it is another plant you don't have to bother with until the flowers have faded. Remove the spent blooms before seed pods can form. In a healthy camellia, this and getting rid of dead and crowded branches is all the pruning you need to do for good flowering.

Many varieties of camellias actually produce more buds than are good for the plant. In nature, these buds would drop off before they bloom. But you can help the tree along by disbudding while buds are still small. The result will be larger flowers from the remaining buds.

Many gardeners will be as concerned with bushy foliage as they are with good blossoming. Page 40 gives this explanation.

When cutting camellias for display, cut the spray of bloom to just above a growth scar, seen here as the ring around the branch below the blossoms. The first ring shows the point from which last year's growth began. Cutting just above it stimulates new side branching.

Flowering Shrubs

Gardenias

Gardenias, noted for their spectacular fragrance, are evergreen shrubs. They blossom best if kept short and bushy, and if the wood is kept rejuvenated. Gardenias bloom on wood formed the previous year, so prune after flowering. Remove the flowers before they start to make seeds. Head the plant back wherever a branch grows higher than 30 inches to keep the gardenia short. Thin overcrowded branches.

If you suspect your gardenia is too tall and thin for the best flower production, get at it with your loppers in early spring before new growth begins. Thin the oldest stems back to 8 inches above the ground, and weak-looking stems as well. The new growth you will be getting now from the base of the plant will bloom in two years. If you keep at this program a few years more, you will be able to get the whole gardenia bush down to the optimum height of 30 inches.

Rhododendrons, Mountain-Laurels and Azaleas

Rhododendrons, mountain-laurels and azaleas, treated in more detail as foliage shrubs in chapter 3, can be made to bloom more heavily by pinching, though in general they do well anyway with little or no pinching. The azalea is sometimes disbudded on plants where large blooms are valued, but it would be a shame to disbud the azaleas whose effect depends on the number of blossoms rather than on their size.

All three plants produce flowers on wood developed the previous year, so pruning is done after blossoming. Pinch off the spent flowers, being careful to leave on the leaf buds that are forming below them. The pinching will cause the number of new stems to increase, and each stem will produce more flowers next summer. On the other hand, if the pruner neglects to pinch and the flowers are left to form seed pods, both new growth and next year's flowering will suffer. Large azalea plantings may have so many blooms that pinching spent flowers is im-

Tall, lank gardenias don't bloom well. The height is usually kept to 30 inches for the best flowering.

practical. Luckily the procedure is least necessary for azaleas, somewhat more so for mountain-laurels and considered really important only for rhododendrons.

Roses

There are many varieties of roses, of which only a few manage to bloom well without pruning. For convenience' sake we will divide the roses into groups according to the way they grow, rather than by variety, since it is the type of growth you want to encourage that will determine how you prune.

For instance, roses can grow as tall or as squat bushes; they can be trained to climb or trail along a support; and they can be massed for use as shrubs or even grown as hedges. Although roses are never strictly a tree, a popular kind of training results in the miniature single-stemmed tree form called a standard rose.

First Pruning: All roses must be pruned when you first transplant them into your garden. If the young roses came with bare roots, the pruning should be more vigorous. Soak the roots in water before planting. Remove them from the water and examine the roots carefully. Cut off any that are diseased, weak or scraggly.

After planting the rose, remove any dead or scraggly branches. Even after the obviously weak or dead branches are cut away, you should cut back some additional top growth in order to maintain a balance with the roots. The amount to cut is a matter of judgment, and depends on how many roots it was necessary to cut. Usually you should leave only 6 to 8 inches of bush above the ground, cutting back the weaker (thinner) shoots in preference to the strong (thicker) ones. Always cut branches back to a bud that points outward. That way you will ensure that next year's growth will be outward from the center of the plant. If any of the cut stems or branches are thicker than a pencil, a safeguard is to apply tree wound dressing to the cut.

Pruning for this sort of display on a rhododendron must be done the year before by snipping off the spent flowers just above the rosette of new leaf buds.

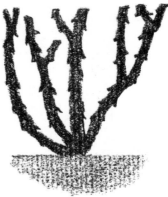

Pathetic as it looks, proper pruning of a rose after it is transplanted leaves you with only a few 6- to 8- inch sticks in the ground. But you will not have long to wait until the side branching and new stems you have encouraged will grow into a more luxuriant plant.

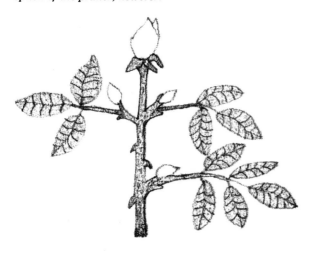

The side buds below the terminal one on this rose stem are destined to be removed to encourage the terminal bud to develop into a large and perfect flower. Disbudding is an option of the pruner, however.

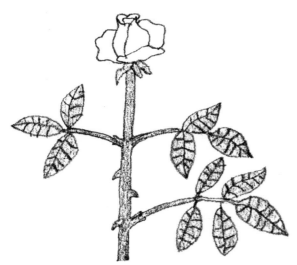

Routine Pruning: After roses have been growing in your garden for a year or more, you will only have maintenance pruning to do. In spring, after growth is under way, check your rose plants and thin them to keep a strong open framework to the plant, so that each blossom receives the sunlight it needs for its fullest development.

Many roses are grafted hybrids. Vigorous suckers which will not produce the rose type you bought often grow from a part of the stem below the graft. These suckers should be cut off immediately, because they will hog the plant's food for themselves and the graft you value will be weakened. Dig below the surface to cut them flush with the stem.

Easily confused with suckers are basal shoots, which are another kind of growth. These too may come from beneath the ground, but they sprout above the grafting point and are the new wood of the hybrid plant. To make sure you do not cut basal shoots off by mistake, check underground to see where they come from if you feel any doubts.

As you get into summertime and buds develop, you will begin to disbud if you want large blooms. Let the bud at the tip of the stem develop and pinch off the other buds lower down the stem. This should be done when the buds are about a quarter of an inch long.

Still later in the summer, when your roses are already in bloom, you can continue to prune in the most pleasant way of all — by cutting flowers for display. Make the cut with a sharp pruning clipper. Leave a stem with at least two sets of leaves. Since buds most often develop near the five-leaflet type of leaf, you should cut back to this. It's even better if you can locate a five-leaflet leaf that points outward so your future growth will not crowd the inside of the plant. Cut fewer or shorter blooming branches from young and recently planted plants. The young plant needs sufficient leaves to manufacture food for continued growth. At this point also some roses are thinned again and headed to shape them while it is still clear which branches have bloomed this summer. But the pruning varies with the variety, and it is best to look it up under our more specific instructions. Finally, when blooms have faded and the plant's energy begins to go into fruit production, snip off the rose hips that are developing, unless, as in the rugosa roses, the hips are decorative or edible.

Bush Roses: Bush roses include such popular varieties as the Hybrid Tea, Grandiflora and Floribunda. The flowers of all of these grow on new shoots that arise from last year's wood. So to catch the plant before it has set its blossoms and while you still can encourage new shoot growth, prune right when leaf buds are starting to swell in the spring.

The spring pruning should start as usual with the removal of dead wood and diseased branches. Then remove up to a third of the previous season's growth. Ordinarily, this would not require you to cut into any wood that has a diameter greater than a pencil.

Check the wood into which you are pruning to make sure that it is green wood. Some wood that is dead can be green outside, but the inside will be brown. If you find brown wood, cut the branch off.

To keep an open center to give enough light to the flowers, the dense growth of bush roses should be thinned. Do this by removing all branches that cross in the center of the plant. Make sure when you head back any shoots that you head back to a bud facing outward.

Shrub Roses: The shrub rose is a particularly durable plant that needs little pruning. Its dense growth, which makes it so useful as a shrub and even as hedges, has only to be kept under some control to prevent sprawling. Thin somewhat by getting rid of the oldest wood and weak-looking stems, and shape them as you wish each year. But head back as little as possible, snipping only those shoots that mar the general outline of the plant. Because of their shrubby growth, you may want to wait until the plant is clearly in bud before pruning, so you can more easily see the dead branches winter has left behind.

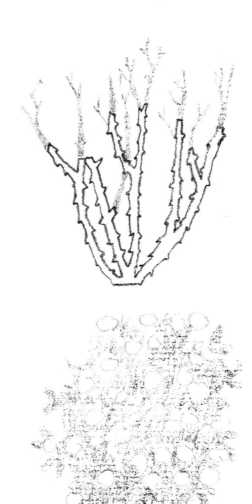

To prune a bush-type rose, remove all dead wood and criss-crossed branches. The plant will grow bushier and produce more blooms.

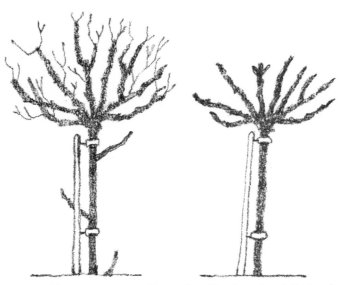

Tree roses are pruned by cutting off suckers close to the trunk and all dead, diseased or criss-crossed branches. This produces both a nicer shape and more blooms.

To get the most blossoms from any of the climbing roses, they are usually trained in a horizontal fashion or in an arch that ends in a downward bend. If a cane is left to grow vertically, it puts most of its energy into getting higher and little energy into producing the new laterals that will carry bloom. But when a cane is bent over sideways – it doesn't matter whether the bend is straight or arched – many "eyes" or buds begin to grow upward along the length of the cane. It is these new laterals that will produce your flowers. If you have trouble getting the canes to do what you want them to, use plastic ties or string to hold them where they belong.

Standard Roses: Standard or tree roses are actually a combination of three plants. The rootstock, chosen for sturdiness, is first grafted to a rose variety that has a strong stem by a method called budding. To this structure the plantsman can bud any of a number of varieties of roses, depending on the particular flower desired. The plant remains somewhat delicate at its grafting points, but that doesn't make pruning any more complicated than with other roses. The objective is mainly to keep a strong circular top, with branches evenly spaced.

First do a routine cleaning out, removing the old rose hips, dead and damaged branches, criss-crosses and suckers that grow from the rootstock. Try to see before you cut a branch whether it is essential to the rounded shape of the top. When you do remove an entire branch to relieve crowding, cut it flush to the larger branch from which it arises. Then cut the remaining branches back, each to an outward facing bud. This heading will increase the bushy lateral growth that not only gives a dense top to the plant, but also more flower buds as the new wood develops. Stake the plant if it seems to need it.

Climbing Roses: Climbing roses, which include the rambling rose, are of two kinds, those that bloom once, and those that are everblooming. The plants are not true climbers in that they have no mechanism for actually attaching themselves to surfaces, but the long, arching canes typical of climbing roses are trained to sprawl gracefully over fences or are tied to trellises.

The pruning of the rambling rose is different from that of any other rose in that only the canes that grew last sumer (or, more properly, the new growth on those canes) will bloom this year. The older canes will never bloom again and so are removed during the second summer after the blooms have faded. This year's canes are trained to take their place, since they are the ones that will bloom the following summer. You will notice that after blooming, the plant sends up long new shoots. These will carry next year's flowers. You can cut all the older canes down to the ground at this point, and tie up the new canes as they get long enough. Since this operation automatically thins the plant, there is no other pruning necessary for rambling roses.

The other climbers are less a special case than the ramblers, because both two- and three-year-old canes will bloom. But as they get older, the canes become less productive and finally cease to bloom entirely. Therefore to get the best bloom, pruning concentrates on removing the older canes after they have bloomed for several years to encourage the new canes that will keep you going for several years more. You might want to prune all climbers about the same as ramblers for the first few years until you get the hang of their growth. You will still get the new canes that will bloom next summer but will avoid the confusion of figuring out which canes have bloomed for two years. When you have gotten more familiar with your plant, however, keep each cane for at least three years. Each year after you have thinned the old canes, head back all those laterals that bloomed this year to buds two or three leaves down from the spent flower. The thinning will encourage new canes to sprout from the base of the plant, and the heading will stimulate new flower-bearing laterals along the older canes.

Flowering Vines

Flowering vines are too often neglected by the home gardener who has a romantic notion that they are best left to nature. What holds true of other flowering plants is true of flowering vines as well. Two good examples are clematis and wisteria.

Clematis

Clematis are deciduous vines that, to the confusion of the pruner, have three different flow-

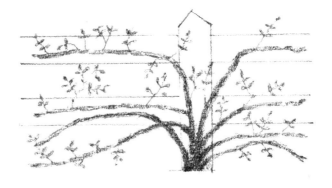

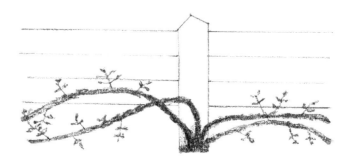

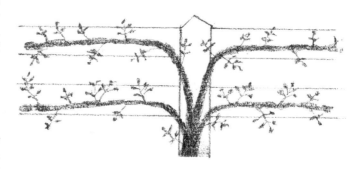

The flower-bearing canes on a rambling rose should be trimmed off close to the ground when the plant has finished blooming in the late summer. Be sure to leave the new canes, which have just grown that year. The new canes should be tied in place after the old canes have been pruned.

ering patterns, each of which requires a different pruning schedule. There is the spring flowering group, like *Clematis armandii,* that flowers on the wood from the previous year. The second kind — *Clematis jackmanii* may be the best known — blooms in summer and the flowers are formed on the new wood that has developed that spring. The third group, typified by *Clematis chrysocoma,* blooms twice, first in spring on the previous year's wood, and again in summer on this year's new wood.

All are pruned both to remove spent flowers and to thin excess growth and crowding. Those that bloom only in the spring are pruned just after they have bloomed so the new wood that will grow will still have time to set next year's bloom. Summer-flowering clematis are pruned either after blooming or in early spring before the new growth from which the vine will flower has matured. It is probably easier to prune after flowering. The clematis that bloom both in spring and summer are first pruned after blossoming only to remove the spent flowers. They are pruned again in early spring just to get rid of excess growth by thinning. In this spring pruning, you'll get the maximum number of flowers if you only cut to the first joint of the previous season's growth.

Wisteria

Wisterias are deciduous vines that are occasionally trained as trees or shrubs. No matter which form you have chosen, your work is not done once the vine is trained (see page 47) because the wisteria is an adamant grower that not only gets out of hand, but sometimes puts its energy into tenacious vine growth instead of into flowers. Prune every year before blooming to keep the vine open to light and air. Thin out laterals that arise from the main stem. Head back new growth by half. On the flower-bearing laterals, remove last year's buds which tend to stay on the vine. Then cut those flower-bearing laterals back to two or three buds. You will get much better blossoms this way.

Perennial and Annual Flowers

Pruning books don't usually include annual and perennial flowers, but since the principles of pruning flowering trees, shrubs or vines can be applied to the non-woody flowering plants as well, you may wish to thin or pinch them as you go about your other pruning. No shears are

It is not unusual for wisteria not to bloom for a few years after planting. Even though it is growing vigorously and producing good foliage, it may fail to flower. To try to remedy this, in the summertime, cut long, straggly growths to a half or a third of their length. This should induce the production of spurs which will produce the flowers in the next season.

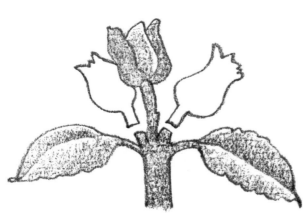

An example of a flower that is usually disbudded to get large blooms is the dahlia. Dahlias are first thinned to two shoots in the spring. Those two shoots are later pinched back just above the topmost pair of leaves when they are about a foot high. The pinching encourages side branches, each of which will bloom at its end. Usually three buds will develop at the end of each branch. When they are still only the size of peas, the two side buds are pinched off and the middle one left to produce a really large flower. You can apply the same process to the taller, larger-blossomed chrysanthemums as well, if you would rather have a few large, showy flowers for decorative use indoors than an outdoor display of profusely blooming mounds.

needed; your fingernails, used often, do the pinching, disbudding and thinning job that flowers need. And you won't have to worry about old and new wood, since all these flowers grow from this summer's stems.

Examples of the kinds of flowers that require heavy pinching are the hardy perennial chrysanthemums, the tender perennial geraniums and the annual petunias. How do you know whether a flower you have needs heavy pinching? By looking in flower catalogs or at good specimen plants on someone else's property. If the heavily flowered specimen is bushy and short and your poorly flowered specimen is rangy and tall, you know you should have pinched. Pinching begins in the spring, long before most plants have set their flower buds. It follows a pattern that is not hard to remember once you've done it a few times. First pinch back the main stem to just above where the first pair of leaves have sprouted. Within a short time, two or more new stems will grow from just below the cut. Each of these stems is now pinched back to just above its first pair of good leaves. Again, new stems will sprout from below the cut. As you can see, this is what in mathematics is called a geometric progression — for every stem you pinch, two more will sprout. How long you continue to pinch is a question of when the plant normally blooms. The fall-blooming chrysanthemum, for instance, is pinched back constantly until the first week of July. The earlier-blooming petunia will be bushy by mid-June, but because it is a constant bloomer all summer long, pinching continues as you snip off the spent flowers.

Examples of the kinds of flowers that require thinning rather than pinching are phlox and delphinium. Here each stalk produces flowers only at its top end rather than from branches. To get the best flowers, some stalks are thinned as they sprout, and the strongest sprouts are kept to develop large, heavy flower spikes.

The thinning on these plants has another advantage. It encourages thicker stalks and may make staking somewhat easier. The delphinium may bloom twice a summer for you if you cut the flower stalks back to 6 or 8 inches after they have finished blooming. New shoots will come up from the base of the plant and, if it is early enough in the summer, may have time to set blossoms. The old shoots can be cut off at ground level as soon as the new shoots are 5 or 6 inches tall.

The chrysanthemum is a good example of what happens when you pinch a branching type of perennial or annual flower. Each pinch is made above a good pair of leaves. Two new stems grow from beneath the pinch.

Routine Pruning Of Flowering Plants

Name	What Wood It Grows On	When To Prune And How
Abeliophyllum distichum (white forsythia)	previous season's growth	after flowers fade, only light pruning for structure
Buddleia alternifolia (fountain butterfly)	previous season's growth	after flowering; cut plants back to two-thirds of original stem to force development of new long stems
B. davidii (orange-eyed butterfly)	current season's growth	early spring, before new growth starts; cut weak stems down to ground
Calycanthus floridus (sweet shrub)	current season's growth	early spring, before new growth starts; head back to encourage new wood growth
Camellia	previous season's growth	after flowering; remove spent flowers; head back to scars where last year's growth ended
Caragana arborescens (Siberian pea tree)	previous season's growth	after flowering; cut previous season's growth back about one-third
Caryopteris clandonensis (bluebeard)	current season's growth	early spring, before new growth starts; cut back to within 4 inches of ground to force growth of fresh new stems
Cercis chinensis (Chinese rosebud)	previous season's growth	after blooming; light pruning to remove dead and aged branches
Chaenomeles japonica (Japanese quince)	previous season's growth or older	either spring or after bloom; cut back new growth by one-third, thin out weak branches
Clematis armandii	previous season's growth	after flowering; prune to prevent tangling
C. chrysocoma	previous season's growth and new wood	after spring flowering; head back to encourage growth later in season
C. jackmanii	current season's growth	in spring; head back to encourage flowering
Clethra alnifolia (summer sweet)	current season's growth	early spring; only light pruning to shape
Colutea arborescens (bladder senna)	current season's growth	early spring, before growth starts; cut back the stems to one-third or one-half length; encourage new stems
Cornus florida (flowering dogwood)	previous season's growth	after flowering; thin to open up structure
Cytisus kewensis (kew broom)	previous season's growth	after flowers have faded; cut back stems that have flowered by two-thirds
C. praecox (warminster broom)	previous season's growth	after flowers have faded; cut back stems that have flowered by two-thirds
Daphne mezereum (February daphne)	previous season's growth	after blooming; needs little pruning; when necessary, cut back to inward-facing bud for more erect plant
Deutzia (all species)	previous season's growth	after flowers have bloomed; cut back flowering branches to stimulate new growth
Erythrina bidwillii (Bidwill coral tree)	current season's growth	before blooming in early spring; only light pruning needed for neatness; remove flower spikes after blooming
Exochorda macrantha (the bride pearl bush)	previous season's growth	after blooming; light pruning to remove weak branches
Forsythia (all species)	previous season's growth	after blooming; remove one-third of stems more than four years old
Fuchsia magellanica (Magellan fuchsia)	current year's growth	early spring, before new growth starts; cut twiggy growth back severely
Gardenia	previous season's growth	after flowering; remove spent blossoms; disbud for larger flowers
Hibiscus syriacus (rose of Sharon)	current year's growth	early spring, before new growth begins; head back each stem of previous season's growth to two buds for fewer but larger flowers
Hydrangea macrophylla (big-leaved hydrangea)	previous year's growth	after flowers bloom; only light pruning to control height and shape

Name	What Wood It Grows On	When To Prune And How
H. paniculata grandiflora (peegee hydrangea)	current year's growth	early spring, before blooming; to encourage current wood, cut to only two buds remaining on stem for larger flowers
Hypericum frondosum (golden St. John's wort)	current year's growth	early spring, before blooming; prune older shrub back to about 1 foot from ground
Jasminum nudiflorum (winter jasmine)	previous season's growth	after flowering; need pinching, thinning, shaping to control growth
Kerria japonica	previous season's growth	after flowering; cut back to the ground old growth that has flowered
Kolkwitzia amabilis (beauty bush)	previous season's growth	after flowering; light pruning for shape
Lagerstroemia indica (crape myrtle)	current season's growth	early spring, before blooming; cut older stems to ground
Lespedeza bicolor (shrub bush clover)	current season's growth	early spring, before blooming; cut down to ground to encourage new growth
Lindera benzoin (spice bush)	previous season's growth	after blooming; light pruning to thin to open up for structure
Lonicera (honeysuckle)	previous season's growth	after blooming; pruning to maintain structure of plant
Magnolia	previous season's growth	after flowering; remove spent blossoms, thin lightly for open structure
Paeonia suffruticosa (tree peony)	current season's growth	early spring, before new growth; cut back all stems to the uppermost healthy bud
Philadelphus (mock orange)	previous season's growth	after blooming; cut back to strong growing bud
Prunus glandulosa (dwarf flowering almond)	previous year's growth	after blooming; remove parts of stems that have had flowers
P. sargentii (Sargent cherry) P. yedoensis (Yoshino cherry) P. serrulata (Kwanzan oriental cherry)	previous season's growth	after flowering; thin for more open structure
Punica granatum (pomegranate)	current year's growth	early spring, before blooming; light pruning to maintain shape
Rhododendron (rhododendron and azalea)	previous year's growth	after flowering; remove spent flowers; remove dead branches; light thinning and pinching
Rhodotypos scandens (jetbead)	previous year's growth	after blooming; only light pruning needed for shaping
Robinia hispida (rose acacia)	previous season's growth	after blooming; light pruning, check for sucker growth
Sorbaria (false spireas)	current season's growth	early spring; cut last year's growth to two buds
Spiraea arguta (garland spirea)	previous season's growth	after blooming; begin pruning for shape
S. billardii (billiard spirea)	current year's growth	early spring; cut back to encourage new growth
Syringa (lilac)	previous season's growth	after flowering; remove spent flowers, periodically remove oldest branches to rejuvenate plants
Tamarix pentandra (five-stemmed tamarind)	current year's growth	early spring; cut back to encourage new growth; leave 2- or 3- inch stubs of previous year's growth
Viburnum burkwoodii (burkwood viburnum)	previous season's growth	after blooming; light pruning for maintaining shape
Weigela florida	previous season's growth	after blooming; prune lightly to maintain plant's shape
Wisteria	previous season's growth	after blooming; remove long straggly growths by about half, except those needed for climbing purposes

5
Pruning For Fruit

High quality fruits are the dream of many gardeners. Yet many people plant an apple tree or blueberry bush, and wait for nature to do her part. You will get fruit by waiting, but you will get more — and larger — by getting out there and pruning. Of course pruning can't do the whole job. The general health of the tree or bush, the soil and temperature and, unfortunately, the bugs and birds control your crop as well.

Because fruits are the final product of a plant's fertilized flower, the basics of pruning for fruit are similar to the basics of pruning for flowers. The flowers you encouraged by thinning to let light and air into the plant are what become the fruit. Defruiting replaces disbudding to get fewer but larger fruits, and attention is paid to whether the plant fruits on this year's, or last year's, or even older wood.

In case of fruit trees, there are two other considerations. One is that apples and some pears, among others, need more than one tree around or the flowers will not be fertilized. A single apple will blossom, but unless your neighbor has an apple tree too, you will not get fruit. No pruning can help you here.

The other consideration is structural. Large fruits are so heavy they may drag limbs down to the ground and even break them. Early pruning during the training of the young trees can certainly help you here. The details of pruning fruit trees for structure are on pages 24 and 25.

Once a tree or shrub is trained, pruning is devoted to keeping the plant open to air and light, and to encouraging the wood from which the fruit will grow.

Fruit Trees

Apples

Apple trees are perhaps the most common backyard fruit tree. The quality of the fruit produced by them is obviously conditioned by the quality of the soil and the temperature and the amount of light it receives, but using good techniques of pruning can also help in stimulating high grade fruit. These days, most apple growers train their trees to a modified leader (see page 24). As the tree matures, many professionals begin to "top" their trees to keep them at a convenient height and to get heavier fruiting. Topping is the annual removal of about a third of the season's growth. Needless to say, the home gardener is not the same as a grower, and this job may be just too much. No matter; you will not get as much fruit as the commercial people, but you didn't intend to go into business anyway. Once your trees have been pruned for structure, your pruning will be an annual routine that to some extent depends on understanding how the apple bears its fruit.

Routine Pruning: Apples are produced on fruit spurs that form on wood that is usually from two to four years old. The fruit (flower) bud is easy to distinguish from the regular vegetative (leaf) buds. It is usually hairy and wider than it is long, and it is wider than the diameter of the spur that produces it. This fruit bud does not increase the length of the spur once it develops. But there is a vegetative bud that is often located right beneath the fruit bud. Its growth is inhibited as long as the fruit is developing, but after the fruit has matured and been plucked, the vegetative bud will develop and form a fruit bud on its tip. This new fruit bud is next year's apple.

It usually takes about five years for the standard apple tree, and two for the dwarf, to begin to bear fruit. It is at this point that routine (rather than training) pruning begins.

The scaffold branches you have chosen previously are maintained by thinning any new branches that grow from the trunk. Suckers, especially the ones that grow from below the graft on dwarf trees, are removed. Occasionally the dwarf trees in particular throw out a thin weak branch that can't support the apples and that fails to bear well anyway. These branches are called "thinwood" and are also removed routinely to favor the stronger branches. As branching begins to get crowded, thin out some of the smaller laterals as well.

Fruit spurs are easy to recognize because, although they may have a few leaves, they are thick, short and marked with closely spaced growth rings.

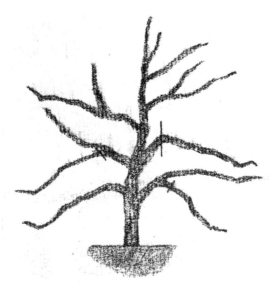

As branches on an older apple tree begin to droop, they are pruned back to a nearly vertical shoot to rejuvenate the tree.

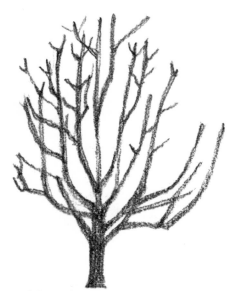

The natural shape of a pear tree is upright and quite tightly branched. It is trained by the modified leader system, but not as radically as the apple tree.

As time goes by and your apple tree grows more mature, it will begin to bear larger crops of fruit. The scaffold branches will gradually begin to droop under the weight of the apples. At this point growth slows and the quality of fruit production begins to go down.

Now is the time to remove the drooping ends of those branches back to the nearest, almost vertical shoot. The reason is not so much structural as it is a question of rejuvenation. The fruit spurs generally have a life span of ten years or more, but after the first few years the number and quality of the apples they produce declines. Pruning back the droopy ends of branches, as well as the routine pruning you do each year, will encourage new growth, new spurs and more fruit.

If as time goes on you feel you have plenty of apples but they are too small, remove some from each spur when they are tiny. The rest will get more nourishment and will grow healthier and larger. In addition, the thinning of the fruits will relieve some of the burden on the structure of the tree.

Pear

The pear tree is usually trained to a modified leader system (see page 24), but more scaffold branches are encouraged because the pear's natural habit is tight, many-branched and upright. The fruits are borne on spurs that live for a long time and grow on wood two years old or older. Most of the lateral growth of the tree is these fruit spurs. Not only do they rarely get too heavy, but if you thinned back the ends of the older branches you would lose the fruit being formed there.

Instead, a pear tree is kept open by cutting back by a third the long, newer branches as they develop, particularly in the center of the tree. This thinning of new wood will keep good light in the interior of the tree and will also force those new branches to develop fruit spurs. Other than this shortening of new wood, the only other thinning required is the usual removal of dead branches, criss-crosses and suckers.

Sometimes pear trees bear excessively. If it worries you, you can always prune off a few fruit spurs.

Peach

The peach tree (and its sister the nectarine) is trained differently than either the apple or the pear. Since the fruit is not as heavy, one can get the advantage of the open center method (see page 24) in which fruits get the best light possible. And unlike the apple and pear, peaches grow only from buds that were formed last summer on that year's new growth. Once last year's branches have fruited, they will never fruit again, so the principal aim of the pruner is to stimulate young growth throughout the tree each year. Believe it or not, this means an annual cutting back of all new growth by one third. Professional growers begin by pruning off all wood that produced fruit the previous year, but if you have no idea which did and which didn't, pruning as you harvest is probably the best method. Pick off the peaches, snip off their branches. Then go eat your harvest and wait until the following spring for the rest of the pruning.

In spring, remove dead wood and thin out the tree in general for light, making sure that fruiting branches are at least one foot apart at the top of the tree. Remove ends of branches that have grown beyond the general outline of the tree, because elongated branches may snap when loaded with fruit. Now cut back one third of all new growth.

When the job is done, you will see much of the tree on the ground. Try not to worry. A healthy peach tree will set large amounts of fruit after this drastic pruning. But the peach is not as long-lived a tree as many other fruit trees, and if the tree does fail at last to respond to your clippers, it is probably time to take it down and plant a new one.

By the way, if you want huge peaches, remove some from the tree when they are still tiny. The others will grow much larger.

Plum

There are three main types of plums found in American orchards today. They are the European, American and Japanese. All are trained to the same open center (page 24) that works so well with peach trees. The fruits of most plum trees are borne on spurs that develop on last year's growth, but produce for six to eight years. Since the spurs are most numerous in the center of the tree, the open center training is just right for letting plenty of light into the fruitiest part.

After the young tree has been trained to three to five laterals with good crotch angles about 24 inches above the ground, little further pruning is necessary. Remove dead, crowded and rub-

The natural shape of a peach tree is broad and low. It is trained by the open center method.

bing wood in the spring, and later cut back some of this season's new growth to encourage the plum tree to put some energy into spur production. If your plums are too small, of course, you may want to remove some spurs to get bigger fruit on the remaining ones.

Apricot

The apricot is pruned quite like the plum. The fruit buds are borne on spurs on the wood of the previous year's growth. In most varieties the long slender new shoots that grow during the summer months will bear fruit the following season. But the fruit spurs that grow on these shoots can be located at different positions along their length, sometimes toward the tip, sometimes along the central part of the shoot and sometimes near the base of the shoot. You will have no problem identifying the fruit bud by its size and roundness. If those buds appear toward the end of the growth, you won't want to prune them at all. If they appear in the center of the shoot, cut back about a third of the shoot. And if the fruit buds appear near the base of the shoot, cut back a half to two-thirds of the shoot.

General pruning will not be very difficult. Thin out enough branches to ensure that the remaining ones will get enough light, keeping an eye on the shape of the tree at the same time. A few varieties of apricot develop fruit on spurs produced on older wood. You will have to notice this for yourself, and be more careful about the older wood you remove.

Cherry

Cherries come in two types — sweet and sour. Sweet cherries tend to grow stiff and upright and sour cherries sprawl more. Train the sweet cherry to the modified leader system (page 24) and the sour cherry to the open center system (page 24) when the trees are young.

Once early training is completed, sour and sweet cherries are pruned the same way. Both produce fruit on spurs that grow from shoots of the previous year's growth. Summer thinning while the plant is young is helpful because it promotes new branching. Thereafter, thin out old wood which no longer fruits to the new shoots that will grow spurs. If you can figure out the arithmetic, try not to thin more than ten per cent of the shoots from the tree each time.

Quince

The quince has been cultivated since ancient times. The fruit is produced from this year's growth so the plant needs little pruning except to keep it from growing too dense. Thin out to let light filter down through the plant. If you don't want to lose any of this year's crop, you can do your thinning late in the fall or early the following spring.

Some people like to structure their naturally shrubby quince into a small tree (see page 82). It is done by selecting one or several main stems while the plant is still very young and cutting the others down to the ground. Lower branches are cut off the remaining stems. A bushy top is encouraged by routine thinning to let light inside and by heading back to laterals frequently. You may find this form somewhat more convenient for harvesting, but either tree or shrub form will fruit well.

Citrus

Citrus trees, which are evergreen, do not generally need as much pruning as deciduous fruit trees. All citrus fruit is borne at the end of the season's growth, so there is no need to prune for wood renewal.

The citrus vary in the amount of pruning they need, the lemon needing the most to control its lank growth. In general the trees are trained to the low-profile open center pattern (see page 24) with upright branches starting about 3 feet off the ground. Branches that sprout from below 2 feet are pruned off. Once training is completed, only maintenance pruning is in order. Thin overlong branches back to a strong lateral or to a main branch to keep the tree or shrub compact. Fruit is borne at the ends of this season's growth. This new growth can be left alone on most citrus trees, but pinch the lemon to keep the tree bushy.

As citrus trees get older, they tend to fill up with dead wood, lose their vitality and produce lower-quality fruit. To rejuvenate, "top" the tree by cutting out the top limbs that prevent lower branches from getting sunlight. Then "brush out" by removing old twigs and dead wood. If you want to go even further, "hedge" by cutting off side branches by 1 to 3 feet. The whole treatment should get new wood started again.

Dwarf varieties of citrus trees may put up suckers from below the graft, which are of course routinely removed.

Figs

Figs produce two crops of fruit a year, the first in spring from last year's growth, the second

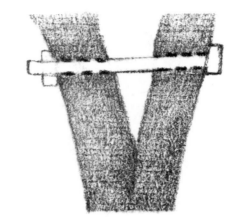

There are two methods of supporting fruit-laden branches if it becomes necessary. Trees trained to a modified leader can have heavy branches cabled to the leader as in the top illustration above. Trees trained to an open center often have their pendant branches supported from underneath by a forked crutch.

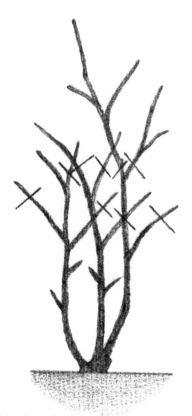

After a blackberry bush is planted, its canes will grow to 30 inches over the first summer. They are cut back to only a foot long towards the beginning of the fall.

The following spring the canes begin to grow longer again and to put forth new lateral growth.

later in the season from this year's new wood. Although the fig can take a lot of pruning, it rarely needs much. After the tree is old enough to produce its first crop, keep any new side branches that emerge from the main trunk and let them grow as part of the basic framework of the tree. As time goes on, thin to encourage new growth, but only lightly so you are not cutting away too much of the wood that will produce figs.

Avocado

Avocado trees are found generally in Florida and California. The trees grown for fruit are usually grafted stock. As a general rule avocados need little pruning for fruit. To insure a strong structure to support the fruit that will appear later, head back the trees when young to get a low and bushy look. This should be done carefully, however. Avocados at all stages of their life have sensitive bark; if too much foliage is removed, the bark is exposed to direct sun and may be damaged.

The fruit appears on new wood, so the best time to prune is just after the tree has produced fruit. Remove dead branches and check the longer lateral branches to see if they might need some support. Dead leaves and branches also appear in the interior of the tree. These should be removed when they appear. Be careful to paint all wounds that are of any size. The avocado does not heal easily.

Fruit Bushes And Vines

Blackberries

Blackberries are vigorous in growth, but much of the growth is not productive of berries, which grow only on the one-year-old canes. Because of this fruiting habit, pruning is mainly concerned with getting rid of older canes and encouraging new ones.

If you are about to start new blackberry bushes, get on your gloves before you are forced to discover how deeply the blackberry thorns can scratch. Set the new plants 3 to 4 feet apart and cut them back to from 6 to 8 inches from the ground. Remove entirely any skinny, weak canes, especially if you suspect they're suckers. By midsummer the canes will have grown to a height of about 30 or more inches. Now cut each cane back to about 12 inches to encourage the lateral growth that will produce the fruits the next year. Sit out the winter, and in the early spring tie those canes up to a wire or loop them over a fence if that's where you planted them. The sun you'll be giving them is good for the berries. Cut the laterals on the canes back to 6 to 12 inches to encourage more new side growth, which will bear the blackberries.

After the canes have fruited, they never will again, so cut them off at ground level. Meanwhile new canes will have sprouted during the summer, and these can now be tied onto the wires or draped over the fence for next year's berry crop. Shorten them, and don't forget to shorten their laterals next spring. Repeat this routine pruning every season and you can expect not only excellent crops, but the least messy plant possible.

Raspberries

Raspberries, which include the common red raspberry and the black variety as well, are pruned much the same as blackberries. Again, fruit is borne on canes that sprouted last summer and which won't fruit more than once. If you are planting new raspberry bushes, you'll have to decide which of two methods to use, "hill" or "solid row." Pruning is slightly different for each.

In the hill method, the plants are planted 5 feet apart and tied up to stakes. In the solid row method the plants are set 3 to 4 feet apart and trained on a trellis or tied along a fence or wires. If it is red raspberries you are transplanting, don't cut back the canes, and don't cut them back at the end of the first summer either. For some reason, cutting back red raspberry canes causes excessive sucker production rather than nice new laterals.

The black raspberry is handled slightly differently. The new canes are pinched back in the summer to stimulate lateral development. Pinch back to about 24 inches if they are tied to a stake, or higher if they are trained on a trellis.

The next year, after those first canes have been harvested, cut them all down to the ground because, like blackberries, they will never produce again. If you have planted in a solid row, tie up this summer's new canes. If you have planted in hills, leave only four to six of this summer's new canes to develop next summer's fruit.

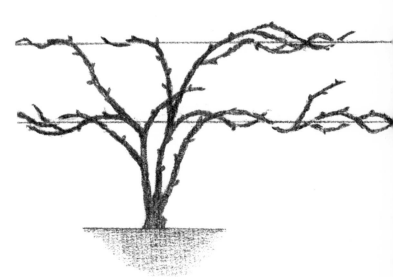

After the canes have fruited in late summer they are cut down to the ground. The new canes that have sprouted during the summer are now pruned and tied to replace the old canes.

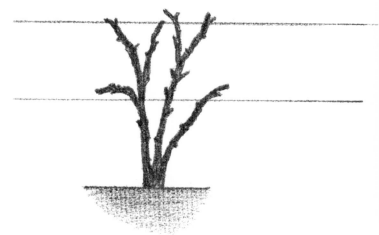

The canes are now tied back to wires, and their laterals pruned to a foot long or less.

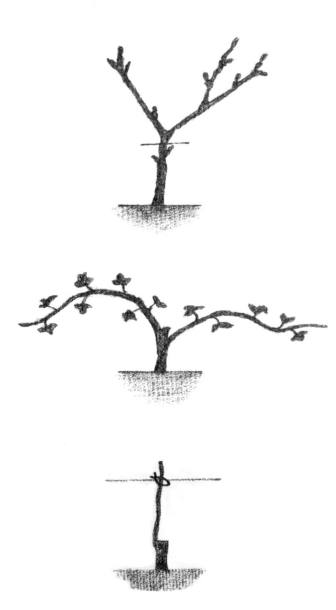

The new grape vine is first cut back to a stem with only two buds. During its first summer, the two buds will become two side branches. The weaker one is cut off; the stronger one tied up vertically.

Next spring, cut the vertical leader back to 3 inches above the wire, and then leave it to grow side branches.

Blueberries

Blueberries develop on wood formed the previous summer. It is the cutting back of this wood to decrease the number of flowers that forces the plant to make the large blueberries that differentiate wild from cultivated fruit. The plant itself grows either as a single-stemmed spreading shrub or as a multiple-stemmed upright shrub. Heavy old stems and branches don't contribute much to fruit production and crowd out light, so one-quarter to one-third of the old wood is the first thing to go in your pruning. The oldest stems can be cut down to the ground. Thin the plant by removing weak laterals and twiggy growth too. Now wait until you can see the flower buds forming, and be prepared for heartbreak. See all those bunches of buds at the end of twigs? That's what you're going to cut off. Cut the new growth of many-budded branches back by half. Cut the shorter budded shoots back to three to five buds each. As the plant gets older, it may be an easier pattern to just cut all twig ends back to the point where flower buds are more widely spaced. Of course if you'd rather have more, but smaller, berries, ignore our advice and just thin.

Currants

Red and white currants produce their fruit from either one-year-old wood or on spurs that develop from wood two years or older, whereas black currants produce their fruit only on one-year-old (last season's) wood.

Both kinds of currants have many stems that sprout both near and from below ground level. More stems sprout than is good for the plant, at least in the eyes of the currant jelly maker. In pruning the red or white currant, cut off at ground level stems that have produced berries for three years, or if you're not sure, whatever looks old. In pruning the black currant, keep new stems that have come up this summer and remove the last year's ones after they have fruited. For both plants, if you see that strong growth has developed at the base of an old stem, you can consider the new growth a stem, and cut the old one back only to that point. Prune either currant late fall or early spring.

Grapes

The grape is the oldest cultivated fruit in the world. It has been grown by man since earliest historical times, and as the first viticulturists must have discovered, pruning is essential to quality grape production. The plants must be trained to some support and then stimulated by pruning to bear large quantities of fruit. Unfortunately, the many varieties of grape have quite different training and pruning requirements, so that what is good for the vinifera grapes grown in California is not good for the Scuppernong grapes of the South or for the labrusca varieties grown in the East. The Kniffen system is the most popular method for training American (fox) grape varieties (which include Concord, Catawba, Niagara, Buffalo, Ontario, Steuben and Interlaken), and luckily it is also the easiest to understand. Many, if not most, home gardeners will be coping with these varieties if they grow grapes at all.

Unluckily, the home gardener who decides to plant grapes will have to wait three years for the first harvest. When you plant grapes check the roots for damage, and prune jagged edges. Allow a good 20 feet between plants along a two-strand wire support, fence or whatever you are using for support. After you have planted the vine, cut the stem back to two buds above the ground. It will look silly, but the two buds will sprout two side branches. When they have grown a while, cut the weaker one off, and stake the stronger one straight up to a 5-foot pole. That's all there is to the first year's pruning.

Next spring tie that vertical branch, which is now a leader, and snip it back to 3 inches above the wire. During the summer, the leader will produce new side branches, but no further pruning is necessary.

In the third spring, choose the four strongest side branches and tie them up along the fence. Prune them back to six buds each. This is what you've been waiting for, because these four branches will produce grapes this summer. But what about next summer? Now is the time to choose four branches for next year too. Locate the four next strongest ones and cut them way back, to only two buds each. Bravely remove every other branch completely.

In the fourth spring, cut off the branches you tied up and harvested the year before, and tie the four newer ones in their place. Again cut them back to six buds each. Choose four others to cut to two buds, and remove all the others. The same pruning is simply repeated every spring.

The third spring, choose four side branches to tie to the wires, and cut each back to six buds. They will fruit this year. Select four other branches for next year's grapes and cut to only two buds each. Remove all other branches.

The fourth spring, cut off the branches you harvested last year, tie up the four new ones you selected and cut them back to six buds. Again, select next year's four branches, cut them back to two buds, and remove all other branches.

6
Hedges

Hedges perform all sorts of functions, from the practical windscreen, to the socially helpful boundary marker, to the just-plain-pretty garden backdrop. In these days of less time for fussy work, people don't plant hedges as much as they used to; they think of all that shearing and abandon hope. We'd like to set the record straight. There are lots of hedges that don't need shearing at all. There are others that look best with a casual pinching now and then. And if you do love that sheared look, there are shrubs that grow slowly enough so the weekend gardener can keep up with them.

If you already have a hedge that's gotten the best of you, read through this section. It may not be as hopeless as you thought. If you plan to start a new hedge, think out what it is you want your hedge to do for you before you dash off to the nearest garden center and buy the wrong shrubs.

For instance, do you want a boundary marker just to convince your neighbor that you're not about to mow his lawn for him, or do you want to screen out his Sunday picnics as well? The first marker could be any low shrub, but the second would have to be tall, dense and evergreen. If you want a garden backdrop to show off your flowers, you might choose to combine the various but unpruned foliages of dwarf evergreens in a pleasing border behind the flower bed rather than worry about trampling the dahlias to prune the rampant-growing privet. The serious isolationist might even consider the trick of a double-row hedge, with wire snuck between the rows to keep out dogs and trespassers. Hemlock and privet are both good wire hiders.

Choosing The Plants

The first thing you will have to consider in planning a hedge is whether the shrubs or trees you choose will be deciduous or evergreen. The advantages of the evergreen shrub or tree are obvious — green and private all winter long. In addition, many of the evergreen shrubs lend themselves particularly well to shearing.

But there is a case to be made for the deciduous hedge. Some bloom. Others are covered with bright berries all winter long. And to many people, the change from green foliage to the tracery of branches is a welcome relief from the solid monotony of an evergreen hedge. Some of the deciduous hedges can be rejuvenated when they get lank by a drastic cutting to the ground — an advantage unknown to the evergreen.

The next division is size. The smallest hedge is probably the germander, technically an herb, but to the gardener it might as well be a dwarf woody shrub, evergreen, shiny-leafed and growing no higher than 10 inches in a naturally neat border. Yes, it can even be sheared to a formal shape. A hedge this size might be enough to remind the children where the garden begins. The tallest hedges are made from trees rather than shrubs, the most impressive being perhaps the deciduous beech or the evergreen hemlock.

Rate of growth will interest you too. Privet, for instance, can be kept as a waist-high hedge, but only with vigilance. An unpruned privet hedge (it's very pretty if left alone, by the way) will grow quickly to 20 feet.

The last basic concern is whether you want a formal type of hedge or an informal one. The difference is real, both in the shrubs you will choose and what they will make you go through in later years. Formal hedges are sheared. You and your clippers must give them frequent haircuts, chopping off all growth that lies within the angle of the shears.

The final shape of the sheared hedge bears little relation to the normal habit of the plant, and shearing can be seen as a mastering of nature. The informal hedge relies much more on the natural shape of the plant. One loses the neat, sharp, geometrical lines of a formal hedge but gains the softer geometry of the shrub's own habit. Upkeep is easier, too, as pruning is mostly a matter of cutting straggly growth as it arises, and pinching new growth to keep the hedge dense. Because this shaping is a less rigorous treatment than shearing, there is a greater choice of shrubs for an informal hedge than for a formal one.

informal type of hedge

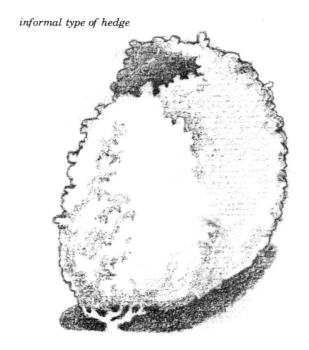

formal type of hedge

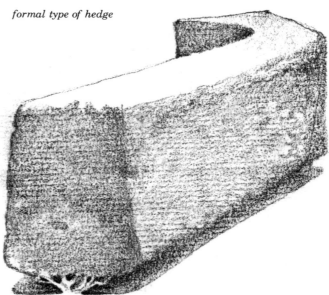

The difference between a formal and an informal hedge is less one of symmetry than of sharpness of outline. The informal hedge will always look softer than the hard lines of a formal hedge.

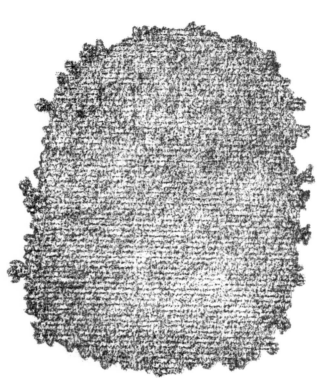

English box is the evergreen that makes the finest smooth hedge, especially for complicated shapes. It is not hardy in the coldest sections, but your nursery can recommend other shrubs that will give a similar look.

Privet is the old favorite. The California privet has lavish growth, and drops its leaves only late in the winter.

Arborvitae is used often for very large hedges since the tall varieties reach a height of 20 feet. There are also dwarf varieties of this dense evergreen.

Taxus, or yew, is evergreen. Its advantage is not only in its dense growth and fresh color, but in the variety of sizes and growth rates you can choose from.

Japanese holly has a nice-sized evergreen leaf that might be of special appeal to you.

Forsythia is an example of a blossoming hedge shrub.

Formal Hedges

Shrubs To Use

All of the following shrubs can be sheared heavily and often to keep them in geometric shapes: privet, box, arborvitae, Japanese holly, yew, forsythia. These are by no means the only shrubs that can be used for formal hedges, but they are among the most commonly used. Before you buy plants for a formal hedge, check with your nurseryman to see which ones will grow best in your area. All the pruning and shearing in the world is not going to help a hedge that's planted where it never belonged in the first place.

Check also to see how large the shrub generally grows and how fast. Your nurseryman can tell you how far apart to space the plants for their eventual size and how often you might have to shear for their rate of growth. We advise buying young plants to train yourself, rather than older ones that, though they'll fill the space better, might resent your efforts to reshape them.

You'll find it's easier to plant your new shrubs in a straight line if you dig a trench (use a string tied to stakes to guide you) rather than separate holes. The loose earth you put back into the trench after planting is going to help the hedge roots along too. The trench should be somewhat deeper and wider than the root balls of the shrubs. To space the plants accurately, use a yardstick or a marked pole. Plant each shrub slightly deeper in the soil than it grew before. Fill the trench up as you go along, water copiously as each plant is in place and stamp down well above the roots of each.

If you want an especially dense or broad hedge you can plant the shrubs in two rows, staggering the plants to fill the space more completely.

Training The Young Hedge

The first pruning is a cutting back, not a shearing. Cut back deciduous plants once they are in place to within 6 inches of the ground. The evergreens need less cutting but they also should have about a third of the plant taken off the top. It may hurt you to cut down these already skimpy babies — the temptation is to let them grow to the final height of the hedge and then try to get them bushy, but it won't work.

The plants will happily grow upward and carelessly ignore their lower branches. The result is something you've no doubt seen many times: a see-through hedge with heavy foliage at the top of the plant only. By cutting down the height copiously now you will get the shrubs to concentrate on producing plenty of laterals, both along their existing branches and as bushy new growth at the base of the plant. That bushy stuff down there is what's going to be the dense bottom of your perfect hedge.

After the shrubs are planted and cut back, they should be sheared two or three times during the summer growing season. Don't allow the shrub to grow any more than an inch or so beyond the last cut you made. The hedge's only defense against your rigor is to put forth more and more small laterals — and that's exactly what you want.

In the following summer, and as time goes on, your hedge will try to get the better of you by growing more at the top than at the bottom. Were you to shear the growth evenly all over, the shrubs would soon be wider above and narrower below. Then the game would get even tougher, because the lower branches, shaded out by the dense top growth, would grow even less and finally die out. So during the first few summers, when you will continue to shear two or three times a season, force yourself to be more severe with the top. Slant your cut inward toward the top so sun reaches the bottom easily, and discourage vertical growth from proceeding too quickly.

Routine Shearing

Once you have the hedge trained, shearing is a fairly simple operation. In the spring have a dead twig hunt with the whole family, because the dead wood that tends to accumulate under hedges is a favorite hiding place for insects that can harm the plants. Most hedges will require a shearing three times a summer, and some even oftener. Check your shears to see that they are sharp and well-oiled; you're going to have a hard time cutting evenly if you're pushing stubborn, dull shears through the twigs. For the same reason don't put your shearing off until new growth has hardened. It's easiest to shear while the twigs are still tender. If your eye for straight lines isn't too good, try using a string line between stakes to guide you.

All the above profiles would be healthy successful shapes for formal hedges. Any of them could be made broader by planting the hedge in a staggered double row.

Informal Hedges

Shrubs To Use

All of the shrubs listed in the formal hedge section can also be used for informal hedges; the softer effect will make them look like quite different plants. But the best news about informal hedges is that you can also use many other shrubs. You can have a flowering rose hedge, a feathery hemlock hedge, a glistening holly hedge, an edible blueberry hedge or a thorny red-berried barberry hedge. What's more, you can use your ingenuity and esthetic sense to plan hedges of different kinds of shrubs planted together in a row. You can alternate evergreen and deciduous, or combine different shades of green, or interweave flowering shrubs with foliage shrubs. Of course, you do have to pay attention to size or the highest shrubs will shade out the lower ones. And you'd do best to get some good advice about spacing from your nurseryman as well.

Training The Young Hedge

Planting and training of the young informal hedge is not that different from the first steps for formal hedges. You won't plant the shrubs so close together as the formal hedge, because the "look" depends on each plant having enough room to express its natural habit. But you will have to cut the height back at the early stages to get dense wood growth, particularly of those lateral branches close to the ground.

Routine Shaping

Since informal hedges use such a great variety of shrubs, you'll have to refer to chapter 3 on pruning for foliage, or to the table on page 48 for the specifics for each variety. For instance, you'll be waiting until after blooming to prune flowering shrubs, but you'll hurry outside early in the spring to catch and snip back Mugho pine candles before they mature. For the most part, though, pruning will consist of removing straggly ends that hurt the general configuration of your hedge, generous pinching back to be sure what you have looks more like a hedge than an overstraight shrubby border, and whatever thinning the particular shrub might need.

The shape of an informal hedge is to some extent dictated by the natural habits of the plants used. The principle of letting light reach the bottom of the plant is maintained both by pinching back top growth and by some thinning of overcrowded branches.

If you have used a mixed planting, the particular blend of shapes may begin to catch your eye in a new way as the plants grow to fill their alloted space. At this point you may choose to keep a certain yew as a very low mound, a forsythia as only a few graceful arches and a Japanese holly as a strong vertical. The more the hedge profile makes sense to your eye, the more it will make sense to your pruning shears. We suggest you do a lot of standing back, cocking your head and squinting your eyes when pruning an informal hedge.

There is still another step you can go in informal hedges — abandon the straight line. Of course you may prefer to call the planting a border at this point, but it is still functionally a hedge. Once you give up the straight line and get more depth to the hedge, you can plan for enough light to include some tall shrubs along with the shorter ones. We have seen what to all intents and purposes is a hedge made of a staggered planting of a large variety of dwarf evergreens.

Informal Tree Hedges

Tree hedges are probably more common in Europe than in this country, but they are certainly worthy of consideration. If you were 20 feet high, there's no reason a tree hedge couldn't be formal, but for most of us midgets the shearing would be beyond us. Any tree that tends to keep its lowest branches all through its life makes a good candidate for a tree hedge. Hemlock and beech are both used for tree hedges, along with the larger arborvitae, junipers and dogwood. Trees like the beech, which normally grow very, very tall, get their leaders removed when they've grown as far as you want them to. Other than that, the pruner must only be daring enough to cut back a half to nearly all the new growth each summer, again getting more severe with the top of the tree than the bottom so that the sides are still slanted inward toward the top. Lopping shears will do the job for a tree the size of a dogwood, but an extension-pole cutter is in order for anything larger. One would usually prune once during the summer, but if you don't get around to it, cutting back the new growth in fall or spring wouldn't hurt the hedge.

Informal hedges can be made up of identical plants to give a uniform look, or can be a mixed planting of either different plants or different varieties of the same plant. For instance, an interesting hedge could be based on the various forms of taxus – the foliage would be uniform, but the outline of the hedge would be pleasingly uneven. The one below is a low hedge of dwarf evergreens.

7
Pruning
For Special Effects

Most of the pruning discussed so far in this book has been of the ordinary keep-your-garden-nice variety. To most people, it is enough to train a strong tree, to keep a shrub bushy, to show off plentiful flowers and harvest good fruits, to maintain a useful hedge. But this chapter is for the fanciful, and it is most likely not everybody's meat.

Special effects pruning is undoubtedly the highest art of the pruner, yet the principles and techniques are the same as in any other pruning. Heading back, thinning and pinching are the main stocks in trade, but here they are used to accentuate nature at her most eccentric, or to defy her altogether. Naturally you must still have a healthy plant; and one whose habit, peculiarity or rate of growth will work with, rather than against, your scheme.

Most special effects can be achieved only by starting when the plant is young. Older shrubs, like older people, suffer from attempts to change their ways. And another word of warning: The decision to try for a special effect represents a commitment to a very regular pruning program. These are not specimens that can be trained and then left alone. You will have to keep after them routinely and thoroughly. If you don't the natural reaction of the specimen will be to try to resume normal growth, but since your training has seen to it that that's impossible, the result is a Frankenstein monster.

Training To A Standard

Training to a standard is when you take what would normally be a multiple-stemmed shrub and force it to become a single-stemmed tree. Examples of shrubs that could be trained to a standard are yew, holly, lilac and box.

On a young plant, select the strongest vertical stem and remove the others. If necessary, stake the stem to support it until it gets stronger. Over several seasons gradually remove the lower branches on the vertical stem. If they are quite large and you fear too sudden a loss of foliage, you can remove them in two stages, shortening them by half or more and then removing them altogether the following year.

Thin out straggly branches each year to get the shape you want and to let some light in. And then head back the branches at the top of the stem to keep a bushy round effect.

Pleached Arbors

This is a very fancy tree-training method indeed, but it results in an astonishing arbor, with laced branches overhead and a double row of unbranched trunks as walls on either side. To pleach, one interweaves the branches of a double row of trees together at a chosen canopy height to form the arbor top. The side branches below the canopy are pruned off in training so that the arbor is open underneath. Any tree can be pleached if it has branches strong and supple enough to bend and interweave. The small beeches, the crab apple and the hawthorn would all work well.

The baby trees are planted in two rows. Each is staked with a long, sturdy pole sunk deep into the ground and reaching to the eventual height you have chosen. Wires are then strung between the poles both the length and width of the arbor. Tie the baby trees to their poles and prune off all the lower branches that emerge from their trunks. As the trees grow and put forth branches close to the canopy, the interlacing begins.

Take the branches and draw them towards the branches of the nearest neighboring tree. If necessary, tie them to the overhead wires. Weave them over and under the wires and neighboring branches. Each year continue to weave the branch ends as they grow and to prune off any growth that goes beyond the arbor height, or any new branches that grow from the trunks below the canopy. Eventually the wires and poles can be removed and the pleached arbor will stand firmly on its own.

A pleached arbor is certainly a big project to take on; but if you have the time, the space and the ambition, it is a rare showpiece of the pruner's art.

Training To Espalier

An espalier is a plant that has been trained to grow flat along one plane or dimension. The word is also a verb — to espalier means to train a plant into any one of many flat forms. For a first-rate espalier a young plant is necessary, since the bending usually required would break the branches of an older tree or shrub. But in some cases — vines, some of the junipers or the firethorn — careful pruning might encourage the plant to yield to your design even after it is mature.

There are two kinds of espaliers, informal and formal. The formal espalier is trained to a geometric shape both by pruning and bending, while the informal espalier is trained to a "natural" but still stylized flat pattern, often without bending. Informal espaliers offer a greater opportunity to use your imagination and the existing branching pattern of the plant to create a pleasing effect.

Plants To Use

Many plants can be used for espaliers. The essential is that they be reasonably small and not such rampant growers that they will grow faster than your clippers can handle. The most popular espaliered trees are the apple and pear, not only because they look terrific in and out of bloom, but also because all the sunlight their flatness allows encourages lots of fruit in a little space. It's easy to pick the crop too.

But fruit trees are not the only fit subjects for espaliering, nor is the following anything more than a partial listing of the more popular ones: Laland's firethorn, Japanese maple, Japanese camellia, flowering quince, Japanese (kousa) dogwood, several of the cotoneasters, winged euonymus, the common fig, showy border forsythia, winter jasmine, Sargent's juniper, the smaller magnolias, crab apple, bristlecone pine, flowering cherry, various yews and several viburnums. If that's not enough, don't forget the vines — flowering hydrangea is a good choice, and most of the euonymus vines.

Many of these plants come in both regular and dwarf sizes. Choose the dwarf for espalier, not only because eventual size is more appropriate, but because the slower-growing dwarfs won't fight back so hard against your pruning.

Informal Espaliers

It is both easiest and most effective to plan an informal espalier pattern around the basic form or habit the plant already has. For instance, the firethorn's naturally arched branching can be accentuated by choosing a single stem, pruning off the others and then encouraging the laterals that arise along the one arch to fan out flat from the curve. Or with a cotoneaster you might choose five or six stems to tie up in a fan against a wall.

To start a new informal espalier, look for a young plant that already suggests some flat pattern to you. Transplant it from 6 to 10 inches from the surface on which you will be training it. The surface might be your house or garden wall, a split rail fence, or two or more wires strung between stakes high enough to achieve your plan. Before you fill in the hole around the roots, check that you have oriented the plant as much sideways as possible, so the major branches are growing parallel to the wall rather than jutting out front and back. Prune off the branches that stick out from behind, since you aren't going to need any growth at all against the wall or fence. Now thin or head back some of the front growth as well, until you begin to see the structure of the plant in two dimensions. Begin cautiously to work on the shape some more. Thin first those branches you know don't belong. If in doubt, head back to a bud that seems to face in the right direction. If it helps you to see things more carefully, or if it is part of your plan, tie the branches back to the wall as you prune, bending them into shape if you want. If you find yourself getting irritated, uncertain or just plain tired, stop. Next year is soon enough to continue.

In ensuing years, you will be pruning your espalier several time a season, heading a bit in the spring, thinning where it gets overcrowded, pinching back enthusiastic growth during the summer and tying as you go. As you get into August you will have to abandon any more pruning, even if the plant is getting a bit out of shape, because you might encourage growth so late in the season that it will not harden before frost and will die back when cold weather comes. If in further doubt about pruning times and methods for flowering shrubs, pines and other special cases, refer back to the more detailed treatment of each in this book.

If you already have an older plant growing against a surface, and if the plant appears to you that it might be espaliered, by all means give it a try, but slowly. Spring would be the best time to start with a deciduous shrub, since that's

Garden stores sell a variety of fasteners for espaliering vines, shrubs and trees. Espalier nails have a soft lead projection that can be bent over a branch without injuring the bark. Plastic tape that comes on rolls is helpful if you are tying to a fence or trellis. Special vine nails are glued to masonry.

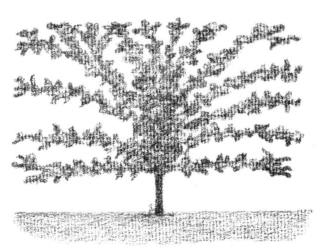

The natural structure of a plant helps the pruner plan his design. Arched branching can be trained to fan out symmetrically, or a single branch may be chosen as an asymmetrical fan.

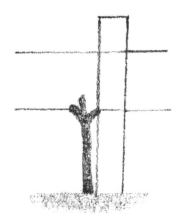

To train an espalier to a double cordon, the first step is to cut the tree back to the height at which you want the first pair of cordons to grow.

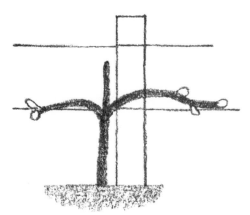

When the tree sprouts new branches in the spring, select a pair for the cordon and allow the center shoot to grow as the leader.

when you can see best what you're doing. Remove the back branches first, shorten or remove some of the front ones and thin out small laterals until the shape comes clear to you. Then remove branches that don't work at all. For safety's sake, wait until the following year to go any further, but then continue as you would with a younger plant.

Formal Espaliers

They say that genuine espaliers offered for sale in nurseries have been trained for about six years, but in our experience most have only a year or two's training behind them. The difference in price is something like 25 to 60 dollars, compared to ten dollars for a baby tree. At that rate you might as well have the fun of the first two years yourself. Look at the pictures of the formal espaliers in this book or others before buying the tree. When you know what pattern you like, draw a little sketch, jotting down the distances you want between the pairs of horizontal branches in the finished pattern. Often you can find a tree that just happens to have branches already at the right places. If you can, you can use the lazyman's method of training rather than the expert's way.

The Horizontal Cordon: The horizontal cordon is the easiest espalier pattern for the beginning trainer. A cordon is simply a branch. Horizontal means you don't have to do any bending beyond the first tying down to make the branch come out horizontally from the trunk. Horizontal cordons are classified by the number of pairs of branches that will be in the final pattern; thus the single cordon has one pair, the double has two and the triple three. Obviously, the more cordons, the higher the tree.

Plant your tree 6 to 12 inches from wall or fence, depending on the size of the plant — say 6 inches for a cotoneaster shrub, 12 inches for a pear tree. Remove branches that grow from the trunk both at the front and at the back of the tree.

Now for the lazyman's method. Cut off all the branches except those that you already knew were in the right place. If you have a real baby, it probably has no more than two of its pairs of branches at this point, and maybe only one pair. Bend these down until they are horizontal (or nearly so, if they resist your efforts) and tie them in position. Snip off any other branches or buds that don't fit your scheme and wait for pairs of branches or buds further up to grow long enough to tie next year. The following year you will begin to tie up the next pair, and to force the first pair more horizontal if you couldn't the first time. Meanwhile, prune off new branches that aren't in the right places along the stem. When you get as high as you want and as many pairs of branches as you intended, cut the leader stem off just where it emerges beyond the highest side branch. That's the basic lazyman's training.

The expert's way is quite different and no doubt gives you a better espalier in the end. After you've brought the tree home and transplanted it, cut the leader at the height at which you want the first pair of branches to emerge. Then wait until next spring, trying to trust that the tree will indeed produce not only the branches you want at that point, but a third branch to be the leader as well. It's supposed to happen, and probably will. Next spring, select the three strongest new shoots at the top and begin to tie back the side pair horizontally and the third shoot vertically if you want more cordons. If you want the tree to stop here, snip off any sprouts other than the pair of shoots you are training to be cordons. Nip in the bud any branches that sprout below the first pair. That year or next, when the central leader grows to where you want another pair of cordons, cut it again at that point. The process is now simply repeated until you get the number of pairs you planned, at which point the extra shoot is snipped off to prevent any more leader growth.

Other Patterns: All the other patterns of formal espalier begin with the same cordons used for a horizontal cordon system. The U-styles call for bending the horizontal cordons vertically when they have gotten long enough. When the top of the U has gotten as high as you want it, just cut what tries to grow beyond that point. Double and triple U's are forced just as you forced a new pair of cordons — by cutting off the branch at the point where you want the U to form and waiting until new sprouts provide you with the two arms you want to train. The Palmette Verrier is only a question of bending each pair of horizontal cordons closer to the trunk than the pair that preceded it, and at a sharper angle than the U. The fan shape calls for training the cordons at an angle instead of horizontally.

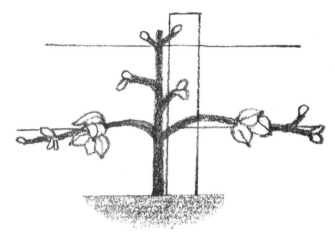

Cut back the leader when it gets to the height from which you want the next pair of cordons to grow. Meanwhile, the first pair has been tied horizontally.

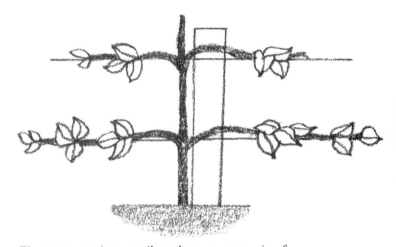

The process continues until you have as many pairs of cordons as you wish. In this case the pruner wants only two pairs, and so he now snips off the central shoot to prevent any further growth of a leader.

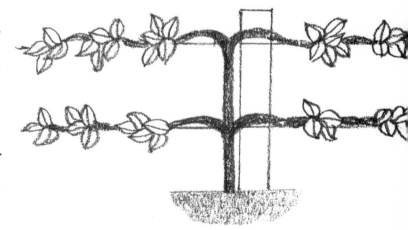

Routine Pruning: Keeping an espalier in shape is better done by pinching or even rubbing off buds than by cutting, since the constant pruning required can leave scars and thickened stumps if you wait so long that shears are necessary. Make it a habit to look at your espaliers every week all summer with your fingers at the ready to pinch off any new growth that is beyond the simple outlines of the plant. Rub off buds along the trunk that would form into unwanted branches. On fruit trees, though, don't snip off the short, ringed fruit spurs that will give you their bounty. As the branches grow longer, fulfilling their pattern, tie them up anew every few inches of growth to keep them straight and true.

Pruning Oriental-Style Conifers

We have been telling you throughout this book to take special care when you prune conifers — particularly pines. They don't grow back well; limbs removed are never replaced. But it is exactly these peculiarities that form the basis of the oriental art of pruning conifers. For here the oriental gardeners have devised an esthetic based on an open and eccentric, often windblown and rugged, look. It is a far cry from the Christmas tree of the Western world.

If you're not already delighted by the prospect of knowing that once a branch is removed it will stay that way, here are some other advantages: the strong accent of a single trained conifer goes a long way towards styling a small garden without creating the shade that another ornamental like a dogwood or crab apple would. You can train a conifer at any age, which means you can save an older tree that has outgrown or overshadowed your garden, or use the method to spruce up a limb-damaged tree by pretending you meant it that way in the first place. But as usual, the best effects are still achieved by training early, especially to get the zig-zag eccentricity that is a trademark of some patterns. The only warning we give on this method of pruning is to look and plan before you cut. If you don't like it afterward, there's nothing you can do about it. If you can draw at all it might be helpful to sketch the design you want before taking out your clippers.

The open style of an oriental conifer artificially creates the look of an aged, eccentric tree.

Pruning For An Open Look

Begin by spreading the branches apart one by one, and removing all the dead wood and all the criss-crossed branches on the inside of the tree. Then cautiously thin out small side branches until the tree begins to look more open and you can see its major structure more clearly. You should probably go into the house now and have a beer or a cup of coffee, find some paper and a pencil, then go out to stare at your tree again for a while. Stare at all sides. Try to sketch the structure as it is now, and then erase those branches you think should be removed. Sleep on your decision overnight, get up your courage the following morning and cut. We hope you like it.

Routine care of your tree should now be done in the spring, when the new growth is still tender. On pine trees, pinch the brand new candles back by half to keep the foliage growing in bushy tufts to contrast to the bare sculpture of the branches. On conifers that have more branching, like the spruces and firs, you have three choices in how you pinch. You can evenly pinch back all new growth when it is tender, leaving a short spur to put forth next year's buds. This method gives an even, bushy growth. You can, instead, pinch off the central shoot at the end of a branch entirely, leaving the side shoots to grow normally. This method adds to the eccentric, irregular look of a tree. Or you can pinch off entirely the side shoots at the branch tips and leave the central one. This last method will give you a smooth, very open and regular look, more feathery than rugged.

Training To A Zig-Zag Look

The routine pruning of an oriental conifer is the basis for a special method of training that can only be used on young trees. As a branch grows — let's say on a fir or spruce — it will grow two side branches to either side of the central growth. Normally, the central growth is longer and will branch out with two more side branches the following year. But if you remove the central shoot and one of the side branches entirely, the remaining side branch will take over. It's the first "zig." The following spring, the zigged side branch will put out two new shoots at its terminal end. This time the pruner removes the center shoot and the side branch

A zig-zag style is achieved by pruning off two of the three branchlets that sprout each summer at the ends of branches. The right branchlet is chosen one summer and the opposite left branchlet the following summer to get the zig-zagged growth on each major limb.

which follows the same direction as the original zigged branch. The remaining side branch, which turns in the opposite direction, is the "zag" — and now you have your first zig-zag. The same process is repeated each year, and the result is that every branch on the tree has a bent, eccentric effect that is highly stylized. Naturally, the tree would look a bit crazy if it had too many crooked branches, so such trees are usually thinned to only the few branches you want to work with.

Shaping Topiary

Topiary, the most fanciful of the pruner's bag of tricks, is the clipping and training of shrubs in three dimensions to create sculpture in geometric and ornamental shapes, including animals, birds and even people. Topiary has been a horticultural art since Roman times, although it's never been very popular in this country. The pruning skills required deserve only the potentially most successful plants — privet, box, yew, arborivitae and hemlock.

Topiary pruning is usually begun when the plant is quite small. Plan the shape as you would for a hedge, sloping towards the top so the bottom doesn't die out. A fat duck, for instance, or a turtle, or an urn, or a pyramid. Keep the growth bushy by lots of pinching, with some thinning of the outermost branches to let light inside as the bush develops.

Gradually, as the plant is growing, shear it into an approximation of the shape you want. Don't be impatient. Getting the final lines may take years. Once a piece of topiary has reached the size and shape you want, constant shearing — probably every other week all summer — is the only way to keep the shape sharp and the shrub bushy.

Since topiaries are often in a humorous vein and this is the end of our book, we offer you that last phrase as a tongue twister. Try it on the next person who offers you advice on pruning.

In the past, topiary was used in very formal ways on large estates, but today it might be more fun to let your imagination loose with fanciful creatures such as the baby elephant topiary pictured here.

Index

hemlocks, 41, 43
hemlock hedges, 80
hemlock tree hedges, 81
Hibiscus syriacus, 49, 64
hill method, 73
holly, 36-37, 49, 82
holly hedges, 80
honeysuckles, 65
horizontal cordon, 86
Hybrid Tea roses, 59
Hydrangea, 49
H. macrophylla, 64
H. paniculata grandiflora, 65
hydrangeas, climbing, 46
Hypericum frondosum, 65

Ilex, 49
informal hedges, 80-81
informal tree hedges, 81
inkberries, 36-37, 49
insects, 11
Interlaken grapes, 75

Japanese camellias, 84
Japanese dogwoods, 84
Japanese holly, 78
Japanese maples, 22, 84
Japanese plum trees, 69
Japanese quinces, 64
Japanese wisteria, 46
jasmine, 49
Jasminum, 49
J. nudiflorum, 65
jetbead, 65
junipers, 32, 41, 42-43, 81

Kalmia latifolia, 49
Kerria japonica, 49, 65
kerry bush, 49
kew broom, 64
Kniffen system, 75
Kolkwitzia amabilis, 65
Kwanzan oriental cherry, 65

Lagerstroemia indica, 65
L. speciosa, 49
Laland's firethorn, 84
lateral branches, 6, 7
lateral buds, 9
lateral roots, 10
laurels, 5
lavender, 49
leader branches, 6, 7, 26
leatherwoods, 48
lemon trees, 71
Lespedeza bicolor, 65
Ligustrum, 49
lilacs, 20, 22, 49, 54-55, 65, 82, 83
Lindera benzoin, 65
Lonicera, 65

loppers, 35
lopping shears, 18-19
Low's ivy, 47

Magellan fuchsias, 64
magnolias, 22, 52-53, 65, 84
maples, 22
mock oranges, 49, 65
modified leader system, 24, 25, 67, 68, 69, 70
mountain-laurels, 33, 38-39, 49, 56-57
Mugho pines, 31, 32, 41, 43, 80
Myrica, 49
myrtles, 49
Myrtus, 49

nectarine trees, 25, 68-69
neglected plantings, 30-33
new wood, 51, 52
Niagara grapes, 75
node, 12

oaks, 22
old wood, 51, 52, 67
Ontario grapes, 75
open center system, 24, 25, 69, 70, 71
orange-eyed butterfly, 64
oriental-style conifers, 20, 88-90
    pruning for an open look, 89
    training to a zig-zag look, 89-90
ornamental cherries, 53-54
ornamental crab apple, 53

Paeonia suffruticosa, 65
palmette verrier, 87
peach trees, 25, 68-69
pear trees, 24-25, 68, 84
peat moss, 22
peegee hydrangea, 65
perennial flowers, 62-63
petunias, 63
Philadelphus, 49, 65
phloem, 10
phlox, 63
photosynthesis, 9
pinching, 16, 34, 62
pines, 22, 26, 40-41
plants
    balance of, 8
    growth of, 8-11
    hormones of, 9, 10
    leaves of, 9-10
    needs of, 8
    physiology of, 8-11
    roots of, 10
    secondary growth of, 9
    stems of, 10-11
    structure of, 6-8
pleached arbors, 83
pleached trees, 20
plum trees, 25, 69-70